CW00482475

FREEING THE INNOCENT

FREEING THE INNOCENT

From Bangkok Hilton to Guantánamo

Stephen Jakobi

Book Guild Publishing

Sussex, England

First published in Great Britain in 2015 by
The Book Guild Ltd
The Werks
45 Church Road
Hove, BN3 2BE

Typesetting in Garamond by
YHT Ltd, London

Printed and bound in Great Britain by
CPI Group (UK) Ltd, Croydon, CR0 4YY

A catalogue record for this book is available from
The British Library.

ISBN 978 1 909984 95 0

Contents

CONTENTS

Acknowledgements

Old men forget. Thank goodness for press cuttings! I have thousands referring to the cases and campaigns during my watch. They cover the whole range of national, regional and local papers from the extreme north of the United Kingdom to Devon and Cornwall. The chapter on the media demonstrates how vital they were to our clients. Whilst the national media would take up a handful of cases when a major event occurred, the local papers and radio would follow every twist and turn in all the cases I was aware of.

Two regional journalists stand out amongst the hundreds I am indebted to for my material. One is Robin Jones of the *Birmingham Evening Mail*. Fair Trials Abroad would never have happened without his support. The second is Joanna Codd of the *Bournemouth Echo,* who took up the cause of Alan Davies from the beginning and followed it for the best part of 20 years. I am also grateful to the great national journalists who helped me: from Nick Davies and Duncan Campbell of the *Guardian* to Frances Gibb of the *Times* and Robert Verkaik of the *Independent*. Then my thanks to all those who made Fair Trials the success it has become. The past Chairs of Trustees, Christopher Bayne and Peter Lipscombe, and all those who served with them. The staff who worked with me, in particular Sarah, Sabine and Patri. I hope that they feel this book has done them and us justice. My gratitude also to those who are currently serving Fair Trials International; Jago Russell and his team.

During Officer training, I learned the Duke of Wellingtons aphorism, 'Time spent on reconnaissance is seldom wasted.' I spent a great deal of unwasted time in taking the masters degree at

Roehampton in creative writing. The decision to write non-fiction rather than fiction was based on that course.

It was Hans Warendorf who encouraged me to write a book which has taken six years and nine redrafts to finalise. Jon Silverman and others read the first draft and gave me valuable advice. My first mentor/editor was Caroline Mylon, local author and documentary maker. Karl French of The Literary Society helped me to make the draft marketable. Carol Biss and all at my partnership publishers the Book Guild, who have believed in my writing: their care and assistance have been invaluable. Special thanks to Anna MacCarthy for her great photographic portrait.

Above all, the clients of Fair Trial. I have strived to make this book about them rather than me. In particular, my gratitude to those who granted me the follow-up interviews. The Coppins, the Daniels family, Diane Toplass, the Shields family and the late Alan John Davies.

Nothing would have ever been accomplished without the love and support of my wife Sally and my children Nick and Francesca. This book is dedicated to my family and in particular my grand-children: Nat, Joe and Sam – may they grow up in a fairer world.

Disclaimer

These memoirs are written by me and I take sole responsibility for the facts and comments in this book. I have taken care with the facts, which I have compiled from interviews, published contemporaneous records and documents. Minor errors may have crept in. I can only apologise.

In particular it should be noted that it is nearly a decade since I had any involvement in the governance or management of Fair Trials Abroad/Fair Trials International. My memoirs are, like all memoirs, history. The organisation has moved on in its views and relationships with others, and a good thing too!

Prologue

'Dad, I'm speaking to you from a locked car boot. They forgot to take my mobile phone off me and I've been picked up and interrogated by the Pakistani security services. I don't know where I'm going.'

In 2002 Azmet Begg had received this call out of the blue from his married son. So far as he knew, Moazzam was living with his wife and children and working with a school in Pakistan, having fled Afghanistan at the first sign of trouble after 9/11. His emotional phone call to me the following year threw me into hectic activity on the Guantánamo issue.

Azmet was a father I could readily identify with: of my generation, a middle-class professional with a son my own son's age. I eventually got to know him a bit. Azmet was the son and grandson of officers in the Indian Army and members of his family had fought for Britain in the Second World War. Whilst he was as emotional as any of the rest of us about his son's predicament, his attitude towards Moazzam's incarceration was reasonable: 'If he's committed a crime, bring him to trial, a fair trial conducted here.' Unlike so many of the families and campaigners involved with Guantánamo, he exuded the avuncular respectability associated with his profession: bank manager.

At the beginning of July 2003, it was announced that six prisoners had been selected to become the first batch of persons to be prosecuted under the new rules. Amongst them were two Britons – one of them Moazzam – and an Australian called Hicks. Somewhere on the way the Americans had concocted Moazzam's confession, which

1

included the risible intention to form some sort of kite bomb (a medieval siege weapon that dropped bombs from a kite over cities) from paper, string and wood and launch it at the Houses of Parliament. I think Moazzam was testing the American military's sense of the ridiculous but in the aftermath of 9/11 the interrogators would believe anything. Hicks, who eventually pleaded guilty and was sentenced to twenty years, had been a kangaroo hunter before he joined the Taliban – a case of poetic justice?

Azmet and I were to work together closely, rousing Britain and Europe, throughout the rest of that year. So many of the turning points in my life have been like that, a chance telephone conversation or meeting with empathy and impulse leading me in a new direction. In this case it was as legal adviser to the European institutions and Moazzam was one of the European citizens released through the personal intervention of the President of the European Union.

Part 1:
Fragments of Autobiography

1

Background and Early Life

My work has made me aware, often uncomfortably, that I am privilege personified: a middle-class, Cambridge-educated, white man with a comfortable home in a leafy part of London and a happy, settled family-life. But it hasn't always been that way.

On occasion, because of a connection with my old college and schools in the East End of London, I am invited to talk to sixth-formers about 'making a difference' when it comes to injustice and unfairness. Looking around the usual sea of bright girls of Bangladeshi origin, I tell them: 'Appearances can be deceptive. Perhaps we have more in common than you think. My father was an economic migrant and my mother an asylum seeker. I was the first member of my family to be born in Britain and use English as a native tongue.'

This is not a hard luck story. My family prospered in England, having left Frankfurt before things got really bad for Jews. We were never poor, and by the time I was old enough to notice, already wealthy. And yet my background explains so much about me and the work I've been drawn to.

In 1933 my mother Gerdy fled Nazi Germany to marry a man she hardly knew. She was a shy and unsophisticated teenager who'd been the poor little rich girl in a highly dysfunctional family of Frankfurt jewellers. She had little experience of the adult world, was isolated from the rest of her family and ill-equipped emotionally to cope with such upheaval. My father, Julius, was fourteen years her senior.

The relationship between my parents was troubled from the start. The gossips have it that my father had been in love with Gerdy's older sister, a glamorous and gregarious beauty, who shared his passion for golf. She broke his heart by marrying the son of a Berlin chainstore empire, so with great pragmatism he settled for her younger sister. Gerdy was introverted, self-conscious – and hopeless at golf.

My father, a shy man, took her off to live in a newly-built housing estate in Ealing. I was born two years later. Julius had come to England from Frankfurt in 1927 to work as the British sales rep for his family firm, Metallgeschaft Jakobi. By the time my mother arrived he was already building an industrial empire with his brothers by melting down pots and pans in the back of a garage on the new Slough trading estate. At the time, there was a huge demand for aluminium in Britain and International Alloys, owned by my father and his brothers, grew rapidly.

In common with so many children of my generation, I rarely saw my father during the war. The Jakobis were producing a vital ingredient for British Spitfire engines and in 1940 my father became senior adviser to Lord Beaverbrook in the Ministry of Supply. He was, at the same time, coordinating the technical and sales side of six industrial plants across the British Isles. He was a rather busy man.

I didn't see too much of my mother either, as she occupied herself working in London with a Jewish refugee organisation. In old age she remembered how important this work was to her and how a row had occurred between her and the Jakobi family because she felt she had to see a group of refugees off to internment during a major Jewish festival.

I was not an unhappy child but dreamy, more interested in books than playmates. I was brought up during the war years by my father's housekeeper, Mrs Bateman, and her husband, a London transport bus inspector. It was Mr Bateman who on his visits to us introduced me to Meccano, then the latest thing in metal construction kits, and together we built a machine gun. Mrs Bateman had a red-headed daughter, Marjorie, living with us who attended the local grammar school and although she was considerably older she played with me from time to time.

In 1940 we moved from Ealing to Gerrards Cross in Buckinghamshire where there was some sort of informal secular Jewish community composed of film directors and businessmen who sent their children to Thorpe House School. It was the nearest thing to a Jewish community that I have ever lived in.

My parent's marriage came to a messy end in 1945, just as the rest of the world was making peace. It was my mother's adultery with Lubo (Aaron Lubowsky), the man who became my stepfather, that precipitated the split, and the laws of the time left her with no rights in the divorce. My father took custody of me, their only child, and I lived with him. He soon remarried the widowed mother of one of my school friends and we were thrown together as a family.

It was a difficult adjustment for a ten-year-old to go from only child to middle son with two step-brothers determined to stake their claim. My older step-brother Peter, who has been a true brother to me for over sixty years, seemed a less than promising sibling at the start. We had serious pecking order issues; he was only three months older than I was but felt he was the man of the house because his father had died in a plane crash towards the end of the war. We fought continually, only stopping for evening doses of *Dick Barton – Special Agent* on the radio. I lost the fights. The whole period was very traumatic.

The time came to pack us all off to boarding school. Having spent his own childhood in Germany, my father knew nothing of the English public school system and took advice from Sandy, a fellow director at his metal company. An ardent sportsman who taught us that work was something you did between skiing holidays, my father was very impressed by Sandy, who had been a silver medallist in one of the 1920s Olympic Games. He told Julius to send us to his old school, Malvern College: 'It's good for sport and sound moral principles.'

Shortly after my stepbrothers and I arrived at Malvern – a mid-Victorian foundation with Gothic main school buildings – Sandy was arrested and jailed for two years for committing fraud at my family's company. I'd have given him longer for that choice of school...

It is the first night at school. The bachelor housemaster retreats behind the green baize door that divides his elegantly furnished domestic quarters, shared with his elderly mother, from our part of the house. I am left in a dormitory of bare boards, naked light bulbs and bunk beds without sheets and blankets. The moment he disappears the seniors put on their black morning coats, seize their silver-topped ebony walking sticks (Sunday dress for school prefects at the time), and silently start to beat me up.

Then I woke up: it was a recent dream brought on by thinking about the school and had its basis in a memory of the prefects' common room of House Number Two, Malvern College, about three weeks into my school career. I was indeed summoned from my sleep late at night to be beaten on my bare bottom with a slipper for failing to recall the incomprehensible nickname for a small school playing field. House prefects took it in turns.

Malvern was a nightmare for a clumsy, bookish boy grappling with growing up. At thirteen, I was one of the youngest boys in the school and dreadfully homesick. The bullying and mindless savagery I encountered drove me into an unnatural shell. The hatred of arbitrary authority that characterised my later life started then, as did the anger at being a powerless victim.

There followed five years of misery and depression while I slowly learned the protective lessons necessary for an over-sensitive and over-emotional boy to survive in such a harsh environment. To me the public school ethos was not based on 'sound moral principles' but the schoolboy code, which has close parallels to the code of the criminal underworld that I encountered later.

Rule 1: Informers were shunned and despised and even if authority picked the wrong culprit for a misdemeanour, *Omertà* (a code of silence) prevailed. If authority couldn't find out who perpetrated the misdemeanour, collective punishment was imposed. In such an atmosphere, morality was defined as what one could get away with.

Rule 2: Perceived weaknesses were exposed and exploited. It was there that I first confronted anti-Semitism and was intentionally put to share a study with an Arab pupil during the 1948 Arab-Israeli war. Up to then, despite having gone through the Bar Mitzvah ritual, I was not really conscious of being Jewish. From then on, it was a major factor in my life. I never pretended I wasn't Jewish, but I had to pretend I didn't mind the institutionalised anti-Semitism at school.

At that time, Malvern was dominated by the muscular Christianity that the then headmaster, Canon Howard Charles Adie Gaunt, preached and lived. It was perhaps surprising then, that one spring Sunday in 1951, at a gloomy classroom in the Great School (main school building), I met a fellow Jew who would change the course of my life. Sir Basil Henriques, a noted philanthropist, came to Malvern to speak about his life and experiences of working in the East End of London:

'You are as privileged as I was, or you would not be here listening to me. It is our duty to plough something back, in recognition of our luck.'

It struck such a chord with me that when it was announced that any interested pupils could meet him in private and discuss matters further, I jumped at the chance.

I had a long talk with him on a one-to-one basis in the head-master's study. It was the first time I'd met a practising lawyer and the first time anyone had spoke to me seriously and in depth about making a difference. He not only enthused me with the good things an idealistic lawyer could do, but we also discussed his work as a magistrate, ensuring that the tramps and drunks that came before him would get shelter and food if they looked really rough.

I never forgot his words – but then, I knew I was going to become a scientist and specialise in metals. At that point, doing anything other than join the family business was unthinkable.

2

Apprenticeship

On a freezing December afternoon, I took the entrance exam for Clare College, Cambridge, and was interviewed by its formidable and eccentric Master, Sir Henry Thirkhill. He gave his best advice to all new undergraduates: 'Always pay cash!' In the South African accent he had never lost he told me my maths wasn't good enough to get a reasonable degree in the Natural Sciences, but he was impressed by my general paper and offered me a place after National Service to read something in the Humanities. My relief at getting into Cambridge overcame any concerns about becoming a scientist.

I was the only member of my immediate family to do National Service, despite my flat feet. My first night in the barracks of the Seventh Training Regiment Royal Corps of Signals, Catterick, was spent writing home for the illiterate half a dozen of my intake. It was my first real brush with anyone who could not read or write.

National Service was just like starting at public school all over again except that this time round I was the experienced one. Because of the compulsory Army Cadet Corps at school, I really needed no basic training and was used by the instructors as an example of how to do things from the beginning. After about six weeks I was singled out for War Office selection board and officer training.

Lunchtime on Thursday, 13 July 1955. I was one of a group of newly commissioned National Service Signallers in a Yorkshire Dales pub trying to get our wireless instructor drunk by plying him with double vodkas.

The radio newscaster announced: 'Mrs Ruth Ellis was executed this morning in Holloway prison for the murder of her lover David

Blakely. . .' In London, hundreds of men and women lined the streets outside the jail in protest, but here, in the pub, the banter continued without pause. I suppose I was the only one who noticed.

I had been following the case as best I might since the sensational trial three weeks earlier. The Times and Telegraph were the only papers available in the Junior Officers' mess; they did not report much about the agitation for a reprieve but we could order the tabloids at the weekends for ourselves, so I followed the campaign in the *Sunday Mirror* and *Sunday People*.

I was shocked at what had happened that day. It was intrinsically wrong that a young woman was killed by the state, by all of us, for something that was clearly a crime of passion. In retrospect it was a forerunner for the Karyn case (the Thai drug-smuggling case that launched Fair Trials Abroad). An interest had developed over the weeks into a passion against the British system of capital punishment and the haphazard reprieve system run by civil servants and home secretaries. This eventually found an outlet in my active membership of the Campaign Against Capital Punishment and my entry into politics.

I'd bluffed my way as a fluent French speaker on the strength of my GCE 'O' level and was seconded to the Allied Land Forces Central Europe headquarters in Fontainebleau as a Duty Signals Officer. We worked a long night shift and during that time I was practically in charge of the headquarters.

My first night shift came before the end of the first week. It was an entirely new experience for me to work with Dutch message clerks, French dispatch riders and Belgian teletype operators. There was also a section of British and American cipher clerks working behind a security section of our communications centre, located in the old stables of the Palace of Fontainebleau.

Each national section had a shift NCO in charge. Holding the whole thing together was a senior warrant officer, usually an American master sergeant, who knew the ropes. I turned up for the shift change at 6pm along with everyone else but the American master sergeant was missing. I had been looking forward to giving the usual order for inexperienced junior officers of all nationalities in these situations: the immortal words 'Carry on, Sergeant.'

I was muddling through the early signals traffic with the aid of the section chiefs whilst frantically telephoning the American quarters to eventually receive the information he had checked out that morning for Paris. Around one in the morning a very drunk American master sergeant poured himself through the doorway and collapsed in an armchair, out to the world. On advice from the experienced British NCO in charge of the cipher section, I telephoned the main gate for the military police. My luck was in; the British were manning the gate and the hapless master sergeant was hauled out of the headquarters under close arrest to await court martial. It was my first experience of European cooperation... an experience that was to serve me well over forty years later.

In those days there were various allowances attached to being an officer overseas and at a major NATO headquarters. In my terms, I found myself rich, able to afford to run my own car and live in my own flat (there was no officers' mess) and join in the background social life of the junior Fontainebleau Armed Forces set. There were no other young, junior, British army officers in the headquarters but there were young naval and air force officers attached to support units and we mixed with French and English civilian secretaries. In particular, I became friendly with a British naval lieutenant who was studying to become a barrister, and we discussed law. It was then I decided to read law after National Service. Through a young Jewish French Officer I learned about the Dreyfus scandal, the nineteenth-century French miscarriage of justice caused by anti-Semitism. I think he was related.

When I left the Army in 1956 the Suez crisis had been building up for months. I had to serve in the reserve for three years and with my experience of working in an Anglo-French headquarters I dreaded a recall. I made a maiden speech in the Cambridge Union pointing out the irrelevance of the Suez adventure and how it was distracting our government from supporting the Hungarian revolution against Stalin. I eventually stood for the presidency and was beaten hands down by John Nott – later to become Margaret Thatcher's Defence Secretary!

Also in my first year, I attended a meeting with Jo Grimond, the leader who initiated the post war revival of the Liberal party, which I joined. It was during this time I read Sir Karl Popper's *The Open Society and Its Enemies*. This seminal political critique of Marx and Hegel, and its promotion of Liberal democracy was voted one of the hundred most influential books of non-fiction at the end of the twentieth century. It remains the basis of my political beliefs.

I wanted to become a professional politician. The consequence was that I joined the lost generation of Liberal Parliamentary candidates and active amateurs. I marched to 'the sound of gunfire' (a quote from Jo Grimond: 'In bygone days, commanders were taught that when in doubt, they should march their troops towards the sound of gunfire. I intend to march my troops towards the sound of gunfire') a total of eight times in various constituencies between 1964 and 1987, much of the time losing my deposit. As a result I am probably the only supporter of the accumulative vote system of electing members of Parliament, which would allow candidates to add together all the votes they got in previous elections.

The brothers Jakobi expected me to come and join the family firm when I left Cambridge with a view to taking over with my cousin John. I had a long discussion with my father and he agreed with my idea that I would be better equipped if I learned about the metals industry outside aluminium circles. I joined the Steel Company of Wales, spending a miserable couple of years in Swansea, cut off from my natural social life. Graduates around my age were either married with two kids or as far from South Wales as they could get. My then girlfriend graduated from Cambridge and moved to London and we drifted apart. I began to realise that I was not really much of a businessman. I made it to London in 1961 and became a manager in the market research department. My social life improved but work was still boring. Politics was much more interesting.

In July 1963, in a dingy Methodist Hall in my first constituency, North Battersea, one of the most beautiful women I had ever seen in my life stood up. She started to harangue me about her experiences in drawing dole money at the local Labour exchange. As a resting, middle-class actress she found it shocking that she was always treated as a VIP and ushered to the front of the queue. It turned out that she was the daughter of one of my committee members, and I managed to invite her out to a totally disastrous evening with both of us vowing never to meet again. An unpromising beginning to the most important relationship in my life. We have recently celebrated our golden wedding.

Sally has always encouraged me to do what is right, rather than what is expedient or popular. She brings to our partnership an emotional stability that I had hitherto lacked and without her I doubt I would have ever accomplished anything.

In 1966, the family business got taken over by a consortium consisting of ICI and the Aluminium Company of America. I was free to do what I liked and Sally encouraged me to become a lawyer, even though we feared our income was going to be almost non-existent for a couple of years. Much to the surprise of my friends, who thought I was a natural barrister, I decided to become a solicitor. In the 1960s, barristers were the Brahmins of the legal profession; they dealt with cases. Solicitors dealt with people and developed continuing relationships with their clients and that was more attractive to me.

At the end of the year I passed my solicitors' finals and obtained articles with Sir Geoffrey Bindman, then a partner in the trade union firm, Lawford, where I got a good grounding in human rights practice. We had a common interest in race relations. In 1965 Geoffrey was legal adviser to the Race Relations Board and I had become, as the Liberal representative on the steering committee of the Campaign Against Racial Discrimination (CARD), the chairman of the Liberal party advisory panel on race relations. At that time we were looking at what became the 1966 Race Relations Act – a great improvement on the 1964 one.

Three particular cases stand out. The first one was one of those very minor everyday miscarriages of justice, rather on the lines of the wrongful conviction for meter feeding, except it left an indelible criminal record on three youngsters' police files. They had been larking around with some uprooted shrubs in the local park when the police pounced. They were charged with vandalism – criminal damage and uprooting the plants, persuaded to plead guilty without legal advice and fined. Their parents were furious when they found out. They investigated and discovered a lack of liaison between the police and the park authorities. The youths had been playing with shrubs that had been uprooted by the park authorities for later disposal, but not yet collected. The parents appealed to the Divisional Court to discover a public policy issue. If someone freely pleaded guilty to an offence, even if they were innocent, the guilt finding could not be undone unless they were under disability. The Divisional Court could change the penalty to a conditional discharge and did so, but the conviction still stood. It was my first and only direct experience of a wrongful criminal conviction that had no remedy in British courts.

The second was that of Beresford Edwards from Guyana, who had found work as a printer in Manchester and become a shop steward for the Society of Graphical and Allied Trades (SOGAT). He was expelled from the union in 1965 for alleged non-payment of dues, consequently losing his job in a closed shop. I spent a week in Manchester, going round with him to take witness statements. It became clear that the only reason he could not get reinstated in the union was the racism of the local branch secretary. We won the case on appeal and Lord Denning denounced SOGAT, ordered £7,971 compensation and concluded his judgment with the dictum: 'A man's right to work is now fully recognised by the law'. Beresford was a big-hearted, charismatic figure who eventually became the father figure to the Manchester Afro-Caribbean community.

The third case was at the Inner London Quarter Sessions, where rising young criminal barristers cut their teeth. It was also an elephant's graveyard for elderly hacks. In a holding cell, a young Afro-

Caribbean, who had committed minor theft offences before but had never been to prison, had just been sentenced to nine months' youth custody for a bang-to-rights burglary. In the background the youngster was sobbing away quietly to himself whilst his barrister, a bright young radical from very radical chambers, was busy ranting on to me about the racially prejudiced jury who'd sent him down. I was mature for an articled clerk – I looked like an experienced solicitor and could talk the talk – but I was at the toddling stage (in fact, I could barely crawl!). The lad had been persuaded by the barrister to plead not guilty and I hadn't spoken out. The barrister thought it was time that the institutionalised racism of Newington Causeway was exposed. I suppose he fancied the case featuring in a suitable article in The Guardian. There was a possibility that a guilty plea followed by a sensible mitigation could have resulted in a suspended sentence and kept the youngster out of custody. No chance of that after the barrister had spent the best part of the day trying to impose on the witnesses his own version of political correctness for the benefit of an unimpressed judge and jury.

The lesson I learned from that is that no lawyer has the right to run his client's case for his own principles… a great acid test to distinguish between real human rights lawyers and those playing the fame game. However, while this was absorbing and worthwhile work it did not provide a living, so I joined a small Jewish firm in Holborn to run the litigation department, and worked for the first British neighbourhood law centre in my spare time.

Allan Jay & Co had two equal partners when I joined. Allan Jay himself had been a world champion fencer and it was a matter of regret to him that he hadn't been at the top of his form for the Olympics. His weapon was the foil, which appeared to me to require lightning thought and reaction, and that is the way he tended to take decisions. It was impossible to imagine him as being capable of working for someone else.

He had met his partner, Bernie Glassberg, whilst he was in articles and Bernie had been his managing clerk. He persuaded Bernie to become a solicitor and Bernie used to tell me he taught

Allan how the law worked and Allan taught him how to become a boss. Soon I become a junior partner in the firm, where I appreciated the opportunity to run my own show within a show. It wasn't an old firm: the clients were mainly drawn from the partners' social circles and extended families. Bernie's clients were East End rag trade and taxi drivers, Allan's fencers and property developers, and mine politicians and legal aid from off the street.

In the early 1970s, my practice changed. A great legal name, Gibson & Weldon, had fallen on hard times and I was approached by The Law Society as to whether I would take over. We changed the name of our firm to Allan Jay & Co, amalgamating with Gibson and Weldon. The firm's sole business was London agency. Major civil litigation was centred in London and provincial firms would appoint a London agent to represent them. The work covered the whole range of litigation from Admiralty (collision between two boats outside Poole harbour) through to taking evidence on Commission (moving the court to hear witnesses locally) in the Isle of Man. There were many solicitor clients ranging from major firms in Birmingham, Leeds and Newcastle to eccentric one-man bands buried in rural Wales.

It was an introduction to major litigation between top FTSE 100 companies, ostensibly about money but actually about chairmen's egos, leaving one with the reflection that if all people were halfway reasonable, lawyers would starve.

My practice began to develop through the London Agents Association, which became the London Solicitors' Litigation Association. I became president of the Association in the mid-1980s. It was a time when presidents were automatically offered judicial appointments on retirement. I had a discussion with the Lord Chancellor's Department about becoming a circuit judge although with my personal views on crime, punishment and the utility of imprisonment, I couldn't see myself sitting as a criminal judge and they weren't looking for civil judges.

We never had much of a criminal practice in the firm. It was mainly careless and dangerous driving, occasional fraud and the odd antique dealer charged with receiving when they got a little careless over provenance and receipts. All this changed in the 1970s, when after Bernie's premature death Alan decided we needed a branch in Hampstead, where most of his property connections worked. I joined the duty solicitor scheme in Hampstead Magistrates' Court. In my day, before the current version of 24/7 coverage, the duty solicitors were the stand-up comedian branch of criminal representation. We covered the magistrates' courts on weekday mornings and had no idea what we would find when we arrived. For example, I learnt on arrival that one of the day's female clients had been remanded the previous week and was due to be represented by a female. With the remark 'I hate blondes', the lawyer was physically thrown out of the cell. I was a bit nervous but luckily in those days I definitely qualified as a balding brunette and represented her unscathed.

Since the accused were not allowed to change legal aid representation without due cause I picked up a wide variety of work: homicides, rapes and burglaries. This included drug mules and heroin users. The sad West African and Latin American condom swallowers were always stigmatised by the press as dealers in death and the poverty stricken wretches, usually mothers with families, were routinely sentenced to eight years in prison. I came across middle-aged heroin addicts still holding down reasonable jobs after thirty years of addiction and came to the conclusion that it wasn't the heroin that kills as such but a wide variety of ancillary activities such as accidents with over-dosage, adulterations and dirty needles.

By 1990 I had become senior partner of my own firm but because of the recession we were finding it tough to make a living. I was earning less than my secretary and mainstream law had lost its appeal. On 19th July, 1990, I was woken up by my usual 6am radio alarm call tuned to the *Today* programme. The first item of news was the arrest of Birmingham teenagers Karyn Smith and Patricia Cahill at Bangkok airport the day before with 33kg of heroin concealed in their luggage.

The *Daily Mirror* headline: WHO WOULD BELIEVE ALL THAT HEROIN? summed it all up. I did not because this weight and street value (perhaps £10,000,000) was far too much for kids. In retrospect, I was well qualified to take the case on. An absolute mistrust of authority and hatred of victimisation from my school-days, familiarity with media and public relations through politics, and with the drunkards' walk of an unplanned legal career, I had gained the necessary experience of the practice of criminal law to become an effective human rights lawyer. Moreover one did not need to be an egotistical monomaniac – but it helped!

Part 2:
Genesis of a Human Rights Organisation

3

The Start of it All: Karyn

My wife used to remind me that when you climb a mountain you keep thinking you're reaching the top, but when you get there you find that there is another peak ahead and then another... This journey was like that. I was fifty-five when I heard about the two teenage girls arrested in Thailand and fifty-eight when I thought I reached the top with their release. So it continued until I retired at the age of seventy-one.

On 19 July 1990, two Birmingham teenagers – eighteen-year-old Karyn Smith and seventeen-year-old Patricia Cahill – were arrested at Bangkok airport when thirty-three kilos of heroin had allegedly been found in their baggage. The event became instant world news. It was the first arrest of its kind and involved the largest amount of heroin ever found in the hands of foreigners in Thailand. What with the packaging, a total of about 100 kilos – where was the forklift truck?

My experience of smuggling had been confined to Nigerian 'mules' attempting to smuggle heroin through Heathrow in swallowed condoms. Relatively small quantities were involved and the women (it was invariably women) were in their twenties and thirties.

Most newspapers that day had photographs of the pair in an airport lounge. There were shots of suitcases full of large bags of heroin, far too much heroin for teenagers. A kilo of heroin was about as much as any serious drug smuggler would allow a drug mule. I thought it would be sorted soon enough by the Foreign Office and they would be sent home.

At the time Sally and I were very worried about our daughter

Francesca, also eighteen and busy traversing the Middle East on her year off. I felt for those parents and was concerned enough to write a letter to the Thai Embassy in London requesting mercy for them. I continued to watch the news. I had no knowledge whatsoever of Thai procedure but it was clear that things were moving toward some sort of indictment and trial.

On August 1st, we went to France on holiday. On August 2nd, Iraq invaded Kuwait, creating turmoil throughout the Arab world. It was a miserable holiday, since we had no news about our daughter. Since the Thailand girls were my daughter's age, the two problems started to get intertwined and I began to get quite obsessed about the Thailand situation. This grew worse as time went on, with no good news coming in.

On the Monday after we returned, I telephoned the Foreign Office and spoke to the desk officer, Ron Dodo, volunteering to do whatever an English solicitor could do to help the parents. I suggested things like putting character references into proper affidavit form and getting them notarised for use in foreign courts.

A few days later, Eric Smith, Karyn's father called me. He was noncommittal. I later found out he'd been warned off me by his MP, a fellow solicitor. 'British solicitors don't do free work,' he'd been told. Two months later I received a telephone call for help from Michael, Karyn's half brother. The Smith family needed affidavits for use in Thailand. Could I come to Solihull?

My daughter had arrived home, safe and well, but by this time I was deeply involved with the plight of the girls.

Sally and I went to Solihull. Eric Smith and his wife Marilyn lived in a well-furnished, three-bedroom semi in the middle of a very long row of similar houses. We immediately took to this handsome, warm, middle-aged couple. They were clearly totally out of their depth and still suffering from shock and bewilderment at what had happened to their daughter. We were introduced to Darren and Sharyn, Karyn's brother and sister. A local journalist, Robin Jones, turned up during the course of the afternoon. It became clear that he was the Smiths' family adviser in the affair. Eric was a

Methodist lay preacher and hospital technician, and had also been a shop steward of his union for many years. The combination of moral backbone and a healthy suspicion of authority were to serve us well.

We talked for hours. Robin Jones had been sent by his paper, the *Birmingham Post*, to Bangkok to cover the story. The chief of the local police and his deputy had admitted to Robin that they both believed Karyn to be innocent and Patricia, the other girl, guilty. I had assumed that Karyn, being older, was more likely to be the leader of the expedition. However, the Smiths showed me evidence that Patricia, although a year younger, had paid the hotel bills and had been in charge of the plane tickets.

So why was Karyn pleading guilty? Eric explained to me that the Thai lawyers had advised that carrying drugs was an absolute offence. It didn't matter whether you knew about them or not. The death penalty was mandatory if one pleaded not guilty but pleading guilty though ignorant attracted a lighter sentence. Besides, no foreigner had ever been acquitted of a drugs offence in Thailand. We were horrified. I agreed to become Karyn's British lawyer and assumed leadership of the campaign to free her.

We learned of the bizarre arrangements at the Thai end. A British woman married to a Thai, Leonie Vejjajiva, had connections with the British Consulate. She had become the Smith's fixer and guide to Thailand. She'd recommended relatives of her husband as Karyn's lawyers and the firm had taken a deposit. After months of inaction, Leonie informed the Smiths the firm had decided to drop the case because they were likely to lose and it would be bad for their reputation. The deposit was not returned.

Leonie had then recommended an American insurance broker friend, John Sobell, who agreed to take on Karyn's defence since one of his employees, Witawat Permaphol, was a Thai lawyer. It was his first criminal trial.

The first problem we faced was to raise money. The Thai costs of defending the case would be around £15,000. A public donations fund had been set up by the well-known British charity Prisoners

Abroad but the fund was not going well due to the public's perception of the case. It had to be changed.

So how does one defend a client in Karyn's situation? I remembered that my friend the barrister, Lord Lester of Herne Hill, had faced the same problem some years before with a Russian dissident. He ran a mock trial through the Western media, highlighting the wrongs of the real court case behind the Iron Curtain. It overcame the difficulty inherent in every criminal defence lawyer's argument without evidence, the inevitable response being: 'Well, he would say that, wouldn't he?'

As our opening salvo, I wrote a letter to *The Guardian*, which was published on 7th December, 1990. In it, I presented the evidence for Karyn's innocence and asked for donations to the fund. Money began to trickle in.

We also planned that on the day of sentence, which was due just before Christmas, I would hold a press conference and release the text of an informal petition for a pardon, signed by Karyn's parents. They would be in Bangkok. The Foreign Office staff were extremely helpful and it was all fine-tuned by local Consular staff in Bangkok. The letter was designed to draw the merits and circumstances of Karyn's case, both to the home public and the Thai authorities.

On Thursday, December 18th, 1990, Karyn was sentenced by the Bangkok court to twenty-five years imprisonment. Witawat had forecast a sentence of twelve years at the most.

The next day I received a call from Sudharee, the information secretary and my contact at the Thai Embassy. She advised me to send the original copies signed by Eric and Marilyn to the principal private secretary to His Majesty the King at the Royal Palace in Bangkok. She even supplied the full address and postcode. Then came the surprise. She told me there would be a pardon on humanitarian grounds, 'you understand,' which could take 'a little time'. In the meantime, I was to keep the matter confidential but could discuss it with British Embassy officials in Bangkok. I telephoned the Foreign Office, who knew nothing of this. They advised me to seek clarification. I sought an urgent meeting with Dohn, the

Thai *chargé d'affaires*. He was on leave over Christmas. A couple of agonising weeks of waiting followed.

The eventual meeting proved difficult. Dohn had obviously not been briefed and had no knowledge of any pardon being promised. Still, Sudharee informed me a few days later that the pardon was on.

On February 25th, 1991, a military coup swept the previous Thai civilian government from power. I contacted Dohn to see if there was any change in Karyn's prospects of release. The diplomat, now fully briefed, told me there was none. Subsequently, two British reporters obtained independent confirmation the promise had been made.

The campaign was still short of money. Although it was some years since I'd last run a marathon I still kept fit with a daily jog so I entered the London Marathon for 1991. The highlight of my campaign for sponsorship was to be one of the three runners to be interviewed by Sir Michael Parkinson on radio. He expressed his amazement at a lawyer describing his client as naive and possibly dim, which is how I described Karyn. I finished in just under five hours but we raised over £3,000.

The Smiths had stayed over in Thailand to be with Karyn through Christmas. Sobell presented a new bill – for £73,000! I offered Sobell the original £15,000, plus a percentage of the income from any sale of the story. He lost his temper on the phone, saying he wanted me off the case and his £73,000 in full. For Sobell, this had always been a game for money.

Another pressing problem early in 1991 was the possibility of an appeal against sentence. Sobell advised we should lodge an appeal, otherwise the prosecution would do so. Both sides duly did. The advice given by Leonie Vejijiva, the Consular fixer, was against this: get the legal proceedings out of the way to get a Royal pardon. The prosecution dropped its appeal. Months later, when Karyn was back in court again for her appeal to be formally dropped, Witawat failed to turn up and she was left to do the job herself.

Meanwhile, the campaign had grown, and we needed an organiser. We were lucky to find Ian Elves, a senior local government worker. He had been to university with Stephen Hughes, the deputy leader of the British Labour group of MEPs. Hughes suggested taking the matter to the European Parliament as a human rights case. I was hesitant because we could be stirring up a row and jeopardising the pardon. Meanwhile, Steve Hughes, quite unknown to us, had organised a write-in by his fellow MEPs, targeting their countries' Thai Embassies. Several of them did so. Nobody received a reply.

There were issues affecting Karyn's health. She had not received inoculations against tropical diseases and typhus was rife in the prison. Meanwhile, the Thais had gone silent on the pardon. We eventually decided to go ahead.

Steve Hughes and Roger Barton MEP invited me to Brussels to present Karyn's case to the British political groups. We drafted a strongly-worded resolution in one of the European Parliament's tea rooms, asking the King of Thailand for action to be taken. I was warmly received by the Labour group. The meeting with the British Conservatives lasted much longer and their questions were more about me and my career than about the case. We discussed my personal politics – I presumed they thought I was some sort of 'Red Peril' and I left the Tory meeting feeling a deep sense of failure.

A few days later, Susan Bramley, an official visitor to the prison, contacted Eric with a tale. The girls had been called into the commandant's office and asked by frantic Thai government officials why they hadn't submitted their application for a pardon. They were told that the applications could be written on a simple scrap of paper.

This looked serious. The problem was it was Friday evening by the time I got the information. I worked hard throughout that weekend to get messages to Karyn and Patricia. I made dozens of telephone calls, beginning by locating Susan who could not get Karyn to do anything. Then I tried to get hold of Patricia's English lawyer out of hours. Progress reports to Robin and Eric. On Sunday evening (Thai time) I faxed Patricia's Thai lawyer on behalf of both girls – there was nothing more I could think of to do. Had there been a window of opportunity caused by all the political activity which had closed due to our inability to get the message through?

October arrived. The motion on Karyn's case was to be debated in the monthly European Parliament plenary session in Strasberg. The FCO (Foreign and Commonwealth Office) wanted to speak to the Smiths and a meeting took place on the very morning we were due to fly out. Implicit throughout the forty-five minute meeting was the priority of maintaining relations with a friendly country. 'Who knows, in a few years we might be able to get Karyn back,' the head of the S E Asian department said. Eric lost his temper and pointed out that the FCO had done nothing. The three of us flew to Strasbourg.

We took our seats in the front row of the public gallery in the main chamber of the European Parliament, Strasberg. The chamber was far more crowded than a normal session of the British House of Commons. They rationed the length of speeches – two minutes for proposers and opposers of resolutions, one minute for everyone else. Even so, the motion-packed agenda dragged on endlessly. Then came the human rights session. Karyn's name was near the bottom of the list. I needn't have worried about the Conservative group, the motion was carried without dissent. The President indicated that the Smiths were in the gallery, and they were given a round of applause by the assembly.

The motion had two direct consequences. The Thai government replied to the first bunch of letters from MEPs. 'Our judicial process commands a distinct place in the judicial world,' was a memorable phrase with which I could only agree. We had also managed to attract the attention of Nick Davies, one of our most distinguished investigative journalists.

Nick produced a lengthy award-winning feature in *The Guardian* on 26th October, 1991. It highlighted the flaws in the prosecution case against Karyn, along with my growing unhappiness with Sobell, his team in Thailand and the FCO. Amongst the flood of letters we received was one which simply said:

'I always thought that if anything unfair happened to me abroad the Foreign Office would do everything practicable to right the wrong. The sad truth is that you are on your own.'

Sobell was so angry he threatened *The Guardian* with a libel action. Nothing came of it.

In November I returned from a three-week trekking holiday in Nepal. To my surprise, I was greeted by a headline on page one of *The Observer* that read, FOREIGN OFFICE WON'T BACK DRUG TRAFFICKER'S PLEA TO THAI KING. What followed must have been one of the most deliberately meretricious articles published in recent times by a broadsheet newspaper. The reader was informed that British Embassy officials in Bangkok 'claim the European Parliament was hoodwinked into passing a resolution calling for Smith's early release, acting on information which was "by and large a fairy tale".'

It went on: 'Smith's Bangkok lawyers say they are concerned by the actions of London lawyer Stephen Jakobi. Smith's solicitor in Thailand, Thawatchai Chaiyasitti, said: "Mr Jakobi suddenly said he was representing the Smith family and raising cash for her appeal. But he instructed us not to appeal the case because he had other contacts. We have not yet received any of the money he has promised."'

The accusations were completely untrue. I had been instructed by the family to raise money for the cost of the whole case and had sent almost all the money I raised to Prisoners Abroad for onward transmission to Sobell. The Foreign Office moved swiftly. There was an official denial of the contents of the article as it applied to them. The ambassador grilled his entire staff to find out who, if anyone, had spoken to the press: no one had.

I really had no alternative but to institute proceedings for libel. I hated being personally involved in litigation. A few years before, I had found myself executor of a family will defending a claim by an aggrieved ex-wife of the deceased. The stress factor gave me sleepless nights even then. During the course of the action, which dragged on for years, we discovered that Sobell had abused Eric's and Karyn's trust by getting her to sign papers to help *The Observer*. It became clear that the real source of *The Observer* article had been Sobell and his associates, although it had been written by an ex-pat freelance journalist in Thailand, Andrew Drummond. There was nothing the defence could prove that was either correct or fair comment in that article. I achieved the official satisfaction of an apology in open court, damages and costs.

By February 1992 it was clear to me, based on court records and Smith family photographs of the containers that the girls were carrying in their cases, that there was a Tardis effect: the containers were far too small for the alleged amount of heroin.

That month a follow-up article on Karyn's case written by Nick Davies appeared in *The Guardian*, under the title BARRAGE OF LIES. He told how Customs and Excise had been briefing journalists, politicians and civil servants about a wholly fictitious record of drug convictions recorded against Karyn. The article caused embarrassment to the Foreign Office, who had accepted the allegations without checking, as Nick Davies had, with the Birmingham police.

There was a crisis meeting between interested MPs and the Foreign Office minister responsible. They were informed that the FO had been misled by Customs and a false assessment of the case had been made. From then on there was a more positive attitude by the government to Karyn's pardon application.

The Foreign Office was not so positive towards me. The mischief arose through the second Nick Davies article. In a letter to the Charities Commission, discussed later and written in 1994, the Foreign Office accused me of attacking Customs & Excise. They obviously thought I was responsible for the article. It is only recently that I realised it was probably connected with two curious incidents that occurred over the next few months.

During the summer of 1992, the caretaker at Swedenberg House,

Bloomsbury, where we had our offices, reported to me that late the previous night he had gone down to the back door to dispose of the day's rubbish and surprised a well-dressed man wearing gloves riffling through the waste paper bins. On being challenged the man had fled. We both thought at the time that it was likely I was being targeted by a newspaper.

Around the same time, I attended a Law Society drinks party, where an official with an interest in Karyn's case told me that special branch were circulating a rumour that I was only supporting her because of my experience with Turkish jails. I had never had anything to do with Turkish jails – that would come with the Manchester United six the following year. The only connection I had with Turkey was a flotilla holiday the previous summer sailing out of Marmaris. The only suggestion I could make at the time to the legal executive was that there was a typo in some dossier – not 'Turkish jails' but 'Turkish sails?'

In May I went to Bangkok with the Smiths to visit Karyn. Columbia Pictures had funded the visit and they wanted an option on her story. We needed the money for the Smiths to continue to visit Karyn. This was despite being threatened by Leonie that if I appeared in Thailand I would be conducted to prison by the first official I came across because of my insults to the King. All the time I was in Thailand, I carried a letter from Steve Hughes, stating that I was on official European Parliament business. Who knows, it might have provided some protection.

The day we arrived civil unrest and rioting broke out – they must have known I was coming. Curfews were ordered. After dinner we stood on the rooftop of a commercial hotel in downtown Bangkok. The entire area was dependent on moonlight. Tanks, passing backwards and forwards on the street below, were the only signs of life. We spent the evening discussing the prospects of the visit. It was the low point of the entire campaign.

Our fears seemed confirmed the next morning. The Women's Prison was closed and we were turned away at gunpoint. It was not until Thursday that I managed to visit the Thai Department of Correction to discuss Karyn, whilst her parents went to the prison. Leoni had been right in a way. I was then taken to the jail after the Thais realised who I was and given the full VIP treatment afforded to a visiting dignitary.

On Friday morning we went to Bangkok Women's Prison. Plastic furniture, 1950s style, filled the diplomats' visiting room. On one side was a counter with a sort of chicken-wire grille, behind which stood Karyn. For some reason, the guards had also brought Patricia to the grille. Both girls wore blue dresses that I understood they had made themselves. They looked well-groomed, pretty girls who would have attracted wolf whistles from any building site back home.

The Smiths talked to Patricia whilst I talked to Karyn. I had never met Karyn before; my impressions of her came from others. Cyndi Lauper's song from the 1980s, 'Girls Just Want To Have Fun' seemed to sum it up before the meeting. My first impressions of Karyn in person were that she was shy and inarticulate. It also crossed my mind that she was really very stupid as well as obviously naive. When I eventually got to know her better it was clearly the artificial circumstances of that meeting that gave me the wrong impression. I was an outsider in a precious family visit and I'm pretty sure Karyn was ill-prepared for my presence. Poor Patricia was an unwanted interloper thrust upon the visit by the Thais in a misguided effort to please. The Smiths and I swapped places. I had professional problems with talking to Patricia and I tried to explain to her that I could not talk to her since she had her own lawyer. Her subsequent behaviour proved she'd never understood this. It was all a mess, really.

While we were in Bangkok, I talked to a number of senior Thai lawyers. The consensus was that Karyn had entered a plea that didn't exist. I found from the meeting with the Correction Department that legal aid was available for foreigners and Thais alike, if they couldn't afford legal fees. It would only be a junior lawyer, but all this was in direct conflict with Sobell's earlier statements, made to both the Smiths and the Prisoners Abroad's appeal. Sobell was formally sacked.

By this stage, we had a pretty good idea what had happened. Karyn was the dupe. She had literally come along for the ride. Her reason for going to Thailand in the first place was because she had wanted to ride elephants. Teenagers who have never been away from home and on their own are not normally given business class tickets by adults to draw attention to themselves. They drank themselves silly. The route chosen was London to Bangkok via Amsterdam with two West African destinations on the way back. I am sure the 'Mr Big' had arranged things so the girls might as well have worn T-shirts with 'Look at us – we're drug smugglers' emblazoned across the front.

Then there was the reward money given to Thai police. International pressure was brought to bear on Thailand in the 1970s because of the country's annual heroin production – around fifteen tonnes – then being exported. The result was the 1979 Thai Narcotics Act which introduced reward money for drug squad officers upon convictions being obtained: the amount of money depended on the amount of drugs found. This could be the only reason why the girls were arrested in the airport concourse before they had a chance to pass through the X-ray machines and why the first news men were on the scene within twenty minutes of the arrest, late at night.

What we needed was scientific proof of the planting of drugs in Karyn Smith's luggage. I obtained it from the Government chemist. His conclusion was that the alleged total of 30.5 kilos had to be total fiction. It was said in the Thai court that the bags of heroin were found inside twenty-one containers including twelve shampoo bottles. That would have meant that heroin had the same density as lead. In fact it has half the density of water. The volume should have filled twenty-one, five-litre jerrycans!

Supporting evidence was piling up from the Bangkok end. A relatively small reward was paid to the police and informers. It was for the equivalent value of under a kilo of heroin in total.

A chance meeting with Anthony Bevins, political correspondent of *The Independent*, led to a front page article at the end of June 1993, questions in Parliament and what proved to be the start of the end game. Hasty arrangements were made behind the scenes to release the girls. On 20th July the girls were sent home.

While Eric, Marilyn and Robin made arrangements to fly out from Birmingham to Thailand to bring Karyn back, I was in charge in England. By 6am I was already conducting impromptu press conferences in the public area of Heathrow airport's Terminal 3 with flocks of media, as rumour followed rumour about the progress of the two girls and their flight. The family party had arrived just too late to bring Karyn back. There had evidently been some argument between the military and civil authorities about their release and the girls had already been smuggled out of the country. The airport authorities gave us the use of a VIP lounge for the meeting with Patricia and Karyn. Whilst I expected Patricia's parents and her lawyer to be there, I was surprised to find that we were accompanied by a couple of drugs squad officers from Birmingham keen to find out what the girls knew about the 'handlers' in the Midlands. I don't know what they thought they were going to accomplish during a family reunion. Surely a telephone call to the lawyers to make an appointment later would have been a more sensible thing to do?

Karyn was cold to me when she arrived. I could understand her disappointment that her parents weren't there to greet her but this was far more than that. It wasn't until days after that I found out that Andrew Drummond, the journalist responsible for *The Observer* article, had been playing misinformation games on his frequent visits to the prison to see Patricia. I did gather while we were waiting that people in the Foreign and Commonwealth Office had held back all the faxes and messages that we had sent to her for the previous month. They were probably concerned about rocking the delicate Thai political situation regarding the pardon. The end result when she met me was she thought I was a meddlesome old fool who had nearly scuppered her chances for release.

So what was the history of that pardon? I believe there had been a decision by the Thai Prime Minister in December 1990 to release Karyn and Patricia at some time the following year, hence the 'promise' of a pardon made by the Thai embassy staff. Unfortunately, the military coup of February 1991 changed all that. The shabbiness of the treatment of the two young girls, who had clearly been duped, had always been known by the authorities. A senior Thai diplomat had said as much to David Puttnam, who had been in contact with us while filming in Thailand early in 1992. It was our exposure of official corruption that did the rest.

But was it our campaign that won their freedom? A documentary series about the role of British embassies' Consular staff overseas featured Karyn and Patricia in jail. It was made under the title *True Brits*. A book, written with the approval of the Foreign Office, was published in conjunction with the series. It heavily criticised me.

'Consular staff ... hoped ... that within a few years, they [the girls] would be quietly repatriated to a UK prison, where, after serving a much shorter sentence than they would have received in Thailand, they would be released.' But... 'Then a lawyer called Stephen Jakobi came out on the scene. His real villains emerged as corrupt Thai police, cynical British customs officers... and, of course, a fumbling and uncaring Foreign Office. The pressure grew to demand a pardon... he eventually persuaded the Prime Minister to ask King Bhumipol to grant them a Royal pardon.'

They said it, not us.

We took Karyn's family to a hotel up the hill from my home in Richmond, Surrey, so that I could stay near her whilst the newspaper bids for her story came in. It was my duty to see what was available and put it to her. A couple of *News Of The World* reporters turned up to my office and pitched an offer of £50,000.

'The girl will be unemployable for years. A sum of money like this in the bank must make common sense,' they said, persuasively.

I am not sure the offer was seriously meant. The reporters started the session by asking permission to run a tape recorder and then wanted to pay my legal fees if I would persuade my client to deal. I refused the bribe.

I remember sitting with Karyn on a small bed in the shabbiest part of the hotel: the management had kindly agreed to put up the family for free until the weekend. She asked me what the snags were. I told her that what they were buying was her signature to whatever they wanted to write. Lesbian hellhole/brutal guards, etc, would make a great story. She said she couldn't possibly allow a story like that to appear in the British papers because her mates in the prison would suffer for it. Whatever doubts I may have had about her innocence were laid to rest at that moment.

Robin Jones holidayed with the family on a caravan site in the West Country for the following week getting her true story. The villains had got her to go on the trip with Patricia on a cover story that they were to smuggle jewellery for refugees out of the country. She was offered £200 to go. As she said, 'For that money, no one smuggles drugs'.

Karyn got married shortly afterwards and had a daughter. She still lives in the West Midlands.

My experience when standing for Parliament in the early 1960s had served us well. In those days candidates had to run their own campaigns, from design of leaflets onwards. The local media and public meetings were major factors in the campaign and television had yet to dominate general elections. What was unique about Karyn's case was the personal commitment. The unease I had felt about the case was translated into a crusade during the course of that first lengthy meeting with the Smith family and Robin. I still remember the anger aroused by their description of the early morning gathering of the media vultures on their front lawn before they really knew what was going on, their only source of information about their eldest child radio and television. The total helplessness of an ordinary family plunged into a crisis with no source of guidance or help, until a local journalist does what he can. From that meeting on, the crusading zeal on behalf of the innocent has never left me.

4

Change of Career (1993 to 1994)

Karyn's return prompted a media fest. There was no way that my partners or staff could get any more work done that week. We were under electronic siege. Our only switchboard was jammed, the fax machine was on the blink and the media frenzy continued right up until the Sunday when the *News of the World* and one or two other papers decided to trash Karyn. I spent most of the time out of the office meeting reporters and keeping tabs on Karyn's debriefing in Devon.

On Monday I returned to the office to find my two partners in a bit of a panic. They must have had a miserable time. They thought that the adverse publicity for Karyn would reflect badly on the practice and we were losing much goodwill. I didn't agree with them, but it was also dawning on me rather belatedly that they didn't share my views on Karyn and didn't approve of the campaign. The whole office atmosphere was poisonous: I don't think a single member of staff was on my side. I was eventually given an ultimatum: drop Fair Trials Abroad and continue to run the practice or retire and become a consultant.

I didn't hesitate. I didn't feel I was doing the practice any good as a rainmaker. The real problem was that we were relatively new, and depended on my contacts in the upper echelons of the legal profession for most of our work. The country had been in recession for the best part of three years. The first phase of a recession is good for civil litigation as creditors go in for massive debt-collecting actions before the debtors go bankrupt. The second phase is when everybody decides the lawyers are too expensive and their solicitors then run into trouble because their clients can no longer afford them. We did not have a bankruptcy practice. Long-established firms have full will chests and people keep dying through boom and bust: the only wills we had were for ourselves and our close relatives. On the other hand there was this enormous unfulfilled need for professional support for victims of injustice.

We parted amicably but they were so convinced that the publicity had been bad for the firm that they changed the name of the firm, left the premises we had been working from for the previous twenty-five years and changed the telephone number, effectively destroying any opportunity for them to pick up my practice. After eighteen months they were out of business.

The Nick Davies article in 1991 had brought a number of concerned volunteers wishing to join a pressure group to support Britons accused of crimes overseas. I had also received a number of requests for help from prisoners and their relatives with cases of merit from across the world. I began to assemble the nucleus for Fair Trials Abroad.

Within weeks of Karyn's return I started up my new 'practice' in my son's old bedroom. I didn't even have a proper desk but was using his built-in workstation/bookcase. I had a combined fax and telephone machine and a handheld tape recorder. In common with most professional lawyers, I couldn't type at a reasonable speed and I was lucky to find Zoe, an extremely efficient audio typist who lived a couple of streets away. She would take my tapes and files once a week turning the dictation into professional-looking correspondence. Anything urgent, including all the faxes, was handwritten. One of the problems of deciphering what I was up to over this period is the difficulty I've always had reading my own handwriting. Faded fax paper only makes it worse. I also acquired a two-drawer filing cabinet. One drawer was filled with the fifty or so thin files that constituted FTA. The other drawer was work from clients that couldn't be transferred. All in all a Neolithic practice.

Initially, I thought I could earn a living from charging modest amounts to people in trouble overseas since I was working without overheads. Legal aid was not available.

I opened for business on November 1, 1993 – and I did not have long to wait for my first big case.

Turkey: The Manchester United Six

On Tuesday, 2nd November, 1993, a large number of Manchester United football supporters arrived in Istanbul for a key European Cup match. About 160 were travelling with the Birmingham branch of the supporters club and had made a block booking with the three-star Tamsa hotel. We don't know what started the riot that ensued. Confused accounts from Turkish sources pointed to a trigger incident in which a British fan masturbated from a hotel window or burnt a Turkish flag (surely not both?).

From 6pm, the story was one of the gathering crowd of Turks in an ugly mood with no police control or attempt to disperse them. From about 10pm the mob started to throw bricks and other objects at the hotel, breaking almost all the windows at the front of the hotel, and then invaded the lobby, trashing the furniture. For about two hours no attempt was made to control the situation until police intervened and drove the locals away. There was then a lull. After some hours the hotel was raided by police, who forcibly ejected all the British residents from their beds and carted them off to police stations spread all over Istanbul. They were then locked up in cramped and unsanitary conditions for more than eighteen hours. Many of the men were kicked and beaten by the police. A deaf, middle-aged woman was taunted about her deafness and a police-man spat in her face. The fans were informed coaches would take them to the match but instead they were driven to the airport and summarily deported.

The group left behind six men who had been singled out for special treatment. The morning after the riot the hotel manager went to the police station nearest to the hotel and picked out these 'ringleaders'. Given that the fans were scattered in police stations all over Istanbul it was quite remarkable how convenient it was to find these six amongst the eighteen held in this particular police station, and none of them to be found amongst the 200 fans held in cells elsewhere. Could this possibly have been something to do with the Turkish law on riots: that it took six people convicted of rioting to constitute a riot, and that the state would not pay compensation for damage unless it was proven that a riot had taken place?

Five of them constituted a complete cross-section of the normally well-behaved Manchester United fans travelling abroad. Their occupations ranged from works manager to tube driver. The sixth man, John Cunningham, was the tour operator. The bewildered six found themselves remanded in custody. On the way out of the remand court they were forced to run the gauntlet: punched and kicked by those lining the way to the prison van. From then on until freed they were subject to casual physical assault whenever they were in police custody for transit. The police were obviously Galatasaray fans. Some officers had joined in the original riot.

Back home when the news broke it was the usual story of the bad behaviour and mass deportation of British yobs. The mood changed on the Saturday when David Mellor, ex-Tory minister and presenter of Radio 5 Live's *Football Special*, found himself talking to an accountant who was icily furious at the treatment he and the other hotel residents had received. Tom Pendry, Shadow Minister for Sport, took the matter up and even Mark Lennox Boyd at the FCO belatedly stopped swallowing the Turkish lies he had been fed through their diplomats.

On Saturday, 13th November I travelled to Birmingham and met with the families and supporters. Even then I suspected an insurance scam. The damage to the hotel was valued at £26,000.

The trial was fixed for 30th November. The proprietor of the travel company offered me a free return ticket to Istanbul. The families agreed that I would go out on 28th of November and, hopefully, return with the six. We agreed my instructions to test out the criminal lawyers and observe the trial.

The trial commenced in Fatih Magistrates' Court, the small court so crowded that I couldn't actually see what was going on. Nor could anybody else, since the television cameras were so intrusive it appeared that the lenses were poking up the judge's nostrils. When I could catch the odd glimpse of him he seemed happy enough: how boring his job must have normally been. The prosecution witnesses were the hotel proprietor, his staff, police officers and one obvious member of the Turkish mob, described as a 'passer-by'. After hostile questioning by the judge, the hotel proprietor admitted he'd been fully insured but had inflated his claim for the damage.

We left court convinced that, since no defence evidence had been needed or called and the six were to be freed as soon as they could be processed, they had been acquitted. We later found out that the case had been adjourned for a week and in the absence of our lawyers the six were given suspended sentences.

Immediately after the hearing I rushed to Istanbul's notorious main prison – the one featured in the Oscar-winning film *Midnight Express* – and waited in the reception hall with my Turkish minder for the prisoners to be processed out. It was still broad daylight but the cavernous hall had little lighting, natural or otherwise. The abiding memory of that brief visit was the nauseating smell. The underlying pong of urine and dysentery was reminiscent of my visits to Victorian British prisons in the 1960s, when 'slopping out' – emptying the cell bucket in the morning – was still necessary. But at least in the UK it was masked to some extent by chlorine disinfectant. Here, it was also dank and clammy. Added to the smell, so the prisoners told me later, were the infested sheets and mattresses. Hot water was confined to a single hosepipe turned on about twice a week with seventy prisoners trying to scramble for it. The only food available without payment was bread and water. Over the next decade I was to visit many prisons outside Europe but for sheer filth and degrading conditions I was never to come across anything quite as bad.

When the time came to render a bill, my expenses and that of my helpers in Turkey included 'vital gratuities'. A month's custody was quite long enough without another night spent in that hellhole. To avoid that we had to pay the prison guards for overtime, and commission a prison van to get the six conveyed to the airport after official prison lock-down.

When we got home I wrote a report, which was widely circulated. The British tabloid pillorying of the defendants had contributed to their being remanded in custody. All foreign governments who are trying Britons in their courts monitor our media and treat the reports as representing British public opinion.

The costs of mounting the successful defence in Turkey and bringing the six home amounted to some £12,000. Only about £4,000 had been raised by collections and donations. I had appealed directly to the Manchester United hierarchy, then – as now – one of the wealthiest football clubs in the world, and they had contributed nothing.

In January we held a huge rally in Manchester. It was an angry, anti-Turkish meeting. Tom Pendry was in the chair and made a magnificent speech about the compensation claim, concluding by placing his hand on my shoulder. 'Of course, everything is now down to our lawyer in whom I have every confidence', he said. 'Our lawyer' felt like crawling under the table.

Afterwards, I made an itemised claim for £370,000 on their behalf. We asked for Foreign Office support in pursuing a claim through the UN. Such a mass deportation and maltreatment of wholly innocent British citizens was quite unprecedented. The MPs involved on our behalf sent us copies of a reply that I characterised at the time as 'bullwash'- a combination of bullshit and whitewash that I was already becoming accustomed to with the FCO. The only remedy that the supporters had was to find a Turkish lawyer willing to run a test case and agree to take a contingency fee. I contacted every Turkish lawyer known to the British Consulate in Istanbul. Only two replied. Both refused. In September 1994, we held a meeting of the claimants' steering committee and it was agreed there was nothing more we could do.

There had been a British police liaison unit in Istanbul which meant a police report. We chased the report up to the Home Office who decided not to make it public. I'm not sure how we found out what was in the report. There had been a 'lost in translation' cock-up. During the lull between the end of the riot and the raid on the hotel, the liaison unit had been contacted by the Turkish police and told that the tour was unofficial. Presumably the British police meant that the tour operator was unofficial, since the Birmingham group were all official members of the Manchester United Supporters Association and holders of officially issued tickets for the game. The Turkish police assumed that the entire group was unofficial and therefore potential gatecrashers and troublemakers. They were fair game.

By March 1994, I was severely out of pocket. The five families who were responsible for the agreed fees and expenses were reluctant payers. I did sympathise with them so I sent them the strongest reminder letter I could think of, threatening them that unless I was paid the curse of Jakobi would fall upon Manchester United and the team would not win the imminent FA Cup Final. It worked. I was paid and they won the cup! Any fan will follow his team through thick and thin. But the Six were real fans. The following season when Manchester United again faced an away match with Galatasaray they all returned to Istanbul.

The case was in fact the prototype for the way I conducted cases in the future, when my clients had funds to pay for travel and accommodation to send me overseas before the trial. Only countries with jury systems have continuous trials and even then some countries such as Italy have a jury system with regular adjournments for up to a month. The extreme is Thailand, where a trial is heard for one day in a month. If, for any reason, such as the scheduled police witness not being available that day, the case is adjourned to the following month. A not guilty plea by Karyn could have resulted in a trial taking years.

So not only are most non-jury trials lengthy, a foreign observer would have to travel backwards and forwards for each hearing and the costs would be prohibitive. I was lucky to cover the Galatasaray trial for the full hearing, but my primary job was usually to assess and often select local lawyers to conduct the case.

There were benefits to working from home. Sally was also working from home and lunchtime was a marvellous time for human company. I was happy to do without the two to three hours daily commute. The downside was my inability to let the answer-phone field calls outside office hours. The psychologists have a term for it – lack of boundaries – and I was often in trouble for running to my office in the middle of the meal. But my overriding memory of that first year was the loneliness of my working life. My professional life had been essentially collegiate. I'd been the expert in my own field but there had always been a colleague who could discuss cases with me. 'The head round the door' when I was in a quandary was something I didn't miss until I no longer had it.

I was also suffering through being a pioneer. British lawyers are used to working in a fair system. For every problem they are ever likely to come across there is an appropriate procedure, a court conducted impartially and a remedy.

Very few British lawyers had any experience of being involved in foreign environments. Cases that arose were almost invariably in Commonwealth countries with legal systems inherited from us. There were a handful of bilingual, dual-nationality lawyers working in two legal systems but no-one was working across the board.

The other major problem was the applicable law. To a working hack, jurisprudence was something that belonged to the academics. They bore the same sort of relationship to practitioners as pathologists to working doctors. After your case has been lost they will tell you why.

International law with its rules on fair trial was something that I last encountered at Cambridge in the 1950s. My memory a mishmash of territorial limits being determined by the range of Canon in the 18th century and diplomatic immunity from paternity orders. I had to buy students textbooks. It was not until 1998, when Amnesty International produced a Fair Trials Manual that collected all applicable law, that the practitioner had readily available access to a single useful textbook.

I discovered that virtually all countries were signatories to unenforceable international law conventions on fair trials. What I was uncovering turned out to be something called soft law. Hard law was national and enforceable, soft law was international and unenforceable.

I was also exhausted. The Fair Trials Abroad work had doubled in quantity and more than displaced the gradual diminution of work needed as a Consultant to the old practice. I had no income to cover the modest outgoings for secretarial help and communication expenses. I used the gradual return of working capital from the old practice to subsidise the new. I was making no headway with Consular support. The only thing keeping me going was the need of my clients. They needed a champion and I gave them a voice.

Yes, all was doom and gloom, but out of the darkness there was that still, small voice saying 'Smile and be cheerful – things could be worse'. An experienced voluntary administrator had just turned up, which meant I would be able to concentrate on the professional side. But I should have remembered the second part of the cynical aphorism. I metaphorically smiled and was cheerful: sure enough things did get worse. I was about to be stabbed in the back.

5

The Assistant From Hell

Phil Cornish told me that he'd run a small building firm which had gone bust in the recession. Since he was a carer for the young handicapped woman he lived with, he decided to look in the voluntary section for part-time work. I was delighted. I had not actually met him before, but when he mentioned he had just finished a six-month contract as PA to Keith Best, the director of Prisoners Abroad, it sounded promising. I invited him to a job interview over dinner at our home and I telephoned Prisoners Abroad for a reference. Keith Best had just left them for another job but the new director told me that Phil had done well and Keith had relied upon him.

Phil came to a dinner interview full of enthusiasm. He was obviously a bit of a rough diamond – not too surprising in a jobbing builder – but of course he knew about elementary book keeping. The next morning I telephoned him and offered him a part-time job as my administrator. I was hoping for a grant of £80,000 from Europe due to start coming in from March. From then on I could pay him a salary.

He clearly couldn't work at my home. Sitting side by side on my son's bed did not appeal, so I managed to find a vacant basement in a council-owned charity building in Twickenham. At last there was somewhere we could park volunteers. Phil would look after the petty cash, administer the volunteers and look after the office supplies. I was the sole signatory to the trust cheques, and it was my money anyway. What could possibly go wrong?

Things started well. He was industrious and full of bright ideas but he was constantly having miseries with his cold damp council flat and had nowhere to go for the festive season. We invited him and his girl to spend Christmas Day with us, putting them in a bed-and-breakfast hotel in Richmond until they could find new accommodation.

Phil seemed to prove himself indispensable as our major link with the United Road Transport Union (URTU), by then working closely with us on lorry driver problems. The union could not give us money as such but they did help us with office equipment. Phil arranged for us to be given a couple of old computers that were constantly breaking down and causing us grief. He also went up North for a week to organise URTU volunteers collecting money for us on the forecourts of motorway petrol stations. By the time we deducted his expenses there wasn't much left for our funds. I put that down to bad luck and bad weather.

In February 1995 I was shocked to be telephoned by a very agitated client who alleged she had given Phil £8,000 in cash to bribe a Thai official so that her son would be released from prison. She accused me of being involved, but when I offered to come with her to the police she refused to allow me to go. She was afraid that if we involved the British police the Thai authorities would take it out on her son. I tackled Phil, who told me she must be hysterical. I did not believe him and spent a sleepless night. The next day was full of emergency sessions with our bank and trustees. The treasurer informed me there was nothing unusual about our bank statements. We were not in a position to charge him with stealing our money. It was our poor and vulnerable client who had been a victim of fraud.

We had no evidence. I couldn't go to the police; it would have been a breach of client confidentiality. There was little we could do but discretely probe other clients when they contacted me. It took months to find another client who had given money and was willing to raise a complaint. We could at last fire Phil for gross misconduct.

The money from Brussels had arrived in the Spring and the trust was solvent at last. In that year the trust was able to clear the bank overdraft of £10,000 secured on my house and award me a salary of

£25,000. I was not to see another salary for a decade. Phil was given a salary of £20,000. He only enjoyed one month of it. During the course of a lengthy police investigation it was found that not only had Phil managed to obtain various sums of money from a number of clients, some of them had made out their cheques payable to us. These clients were initially suspicious of me, which is why I had not been contacted. A number had contacted the FCO, who also had not contacted me. The allegations only surfaced in a FCO letter to the Charity Commissioners of the following year.

There had to be another bank account in our name somewhere. Surely it could not be with our bank? It took about a year to discover that Phil had managed to open a Fair Trials client account with himself as sole signatory at the same branch of Barclay's Bank that we used. The bank never explained to us how this could have happened and why they failed to disclose it at our meeting. Between November 1994 and March 1995, £15,000 had passed through this account – about twice as much as passed through the trust's ordinary account over the same period.

Slowly the investigation uncovered a trail of criminal activity. Phil was a professional criminal with previous convictions for fraud and false accounting (this was in the era before charities were allowed to search for such records). He had defrauded Prisoners Abroad but his fraud had not been uncovered until after we had fired him. It turned out both of us had suffered an 'Aladdin' fraud: new lamps for old. He had bought new computers for Prisoners Abroad and switched them in part exchange for old computers, pocketing the difference. He had played the same game on us. URTU had in fact supplied us with new computers.

Then there were the telephone accounts. A bill for unauthorised telephone calls arrived from BT in July 1995 for over £400 in the last quarter. Phil had also managed to manoeuvre himself into a mobile phone agreement and the next month I received a mobile phone bill for nearly £2,000. The subsequent police investigation showed that these had been mainly calls to 901 sex chat lines in the Philippines and West Africa.

Over the course of time, the police investigation broadened out to include the United States, continental Europe and Asia. The case took over two years to come to trial and as I prepared for it I was summoned to come to court bringing the client files. A hearing date was given to me but I had to apply at short notice to get an adjournment since I was due to go to Bulgaria with the BBC for Hobbs and Mills (two truckers arrested for drug smuggling on the Turkish-Bulgarian frontier). Phil was present in court on my application. On the vacated hearing date, two rough looking men parked opposite my house, which Sally noticed when she returned home from walking the dog. About half an hour later the two men came to the door and asked to speak with me. They left, but Sally was frightened enough to contact the police officer in charge of the investigation. On my return a couple of days later I noticed that the filing cabinet I kept at the back of my open garage had been broken into and the files had been disturbed. I have no doubt that this was an attempt to steal vital evidence and discredit me as a witness through inability to bring the files to court. Those particular files were kept for safety, along with the open case files, in my study, but the episode made us so uneasy we took to locking the garden gate.

Phil Cornish was brought to trial at Snaresbrook Crown Court in December 1997. I was a principal witness. I was very concerned about giving evidence: I was afraid of losing my temper about Phil whilst giving evidence and discrediting myself. I only let the mask slip once – quite a feat during my three days in the witness box.

Witnesses are not allowed into court until they've given evidence. The only way I could compile a report to the trustees was to send my senior member of staff, Sarah, to court as an observer. I arrived at Snaresbrook on my second day having left home at 6am and had breakfast in the court cafe.

Phil's counsel commenced cross examination. This started oddly.

'Mr. Jakobi, you are aware that witnesses must not talk to the press whilst they are giving evidence?'

'Yes, of course.'

50

'So why were you seen having breakfast this morning with that lady on the Press bench?' he continued, pointing at Sarah.

It's a cardinal rule of cross-examination that you must never ask a question unless you already know the answer. Phil must have spotted us in the canteen and jumped to conclusions.

On 26th February, 1998, Phil was convicted on ten of the fifteen counts of theft he was charged with and sentenced to three years imprisonment. I attended the sentencing session to deal with the inevitable publicity involved, but luckily the press was kind to us and made it quite clear, through printing Phil's history with Prisoners Abroad, that we were both innocent dupes of a clever but heartless conman. Years of anger and anxiety had come to an end.

6

The Virtual Office (1995–1999)

I also searched for that elusive attribution for Fair Trials – respectability. From the outset I was determined to continue to hold a practising certificate as a solicitor and to run my outfit in accordance with the principles and ethics of my profession. I couldn't find any umbrella organisation in the United Kingdom, but there was a Francophone one. The International Federation of Human Rights was Paris-based but willing to accept outsiders. What was curious about FIDH was the opaqueness of its financial backers. Then, as now, the source of its million pound budget was undisclosed. After attending a conference in Paris, I found it to be a French government agency: not the sort of thing that I wished us to be associated with, so I dropped out. I have never agreed that NGOs should be dependent on government money.

From the very beginning, I was concerned with being publicly caught out supporting a plainly guilty prisoner. I firmly believe that it is better for the innocent to be acquitted, than the guilty convicted, but too many mistakes in assessment would have ruined our reputation for integrity. I had barely sat down in my son's bedroom when I received a letter from a prisoner in Longueville, the notorious French frontier prison.

'Dear Mr. Jakobi, I know you will hardly credit this but look what happened to me! I was on a bus crossing the Franco-Belgian frontier, and had just arrived in France when French Customs, searching the hold of the bus, found a bag of amphetamine tablets with no labels or fingerprints on the bag. There were thirty-two other passengers but they let everyone off except for me and after a farcical trial, I am in this prison...'

I think he forgot that in criminal lawyer terms I may have been born yesterday, but early in the morning. So I wrote back: 'As criminal lawyers hate unpleasant surprises, I wonder if, by any chance, you have any previous convictions?'

I received this letter back:

'By an incredible coincidence, I had just been released the previous morning from a Belgian prison after having been most unjustly convicted of smuggling amphetamine tablets...'

The thing we dreaded most was the client who failed the 'off the plane' test. A client for whom we obtained early release arrives in Heathrow or Gatwick and announces to the airport media: 'What a relief to be home. The first six trips were okay, but that seventh was a real bummer.' That did happen to me once in the early days.

Samantha Slater, a 25-year-old model from Birmingham, was serving 10 years 'rigorous imprisonment' in Kerala, India. She was sentenced after being caught in possession of one ounce of cannabis, which she maintained was planted on her. A reporter for a woman's magazine after interviewing her in jail was convinced of her innocence and enlisted me in a campaign to free her. After arriving home she failed the test, confessing that she had the cannabis on her when she was arrested.

The other aid to respectability and funding was to become a trust. In the summer of 1994 I contacted friends, relatives and neighbours searching for people who were willing to become trustees. The Treaty of Maastricht had created the concept of European Union citizenship in 1992. There were lots of good reasons for becoming a European Union citizens' organisation. I didn't want to get involved in immigration/alien cases. It was far more straightforward to be able to put pressure on the individual's MP and one could involve the European Parliament and Commission to get concerned about the rights of European citizens. Also it was vital to get steady core funding from a single source. In my trips to Brussels I had sounded out influential members of the European Parliament and the

Commission and discovered that there were substantial funds available to organisations such as ours but I needed a collection of fellow Europhiles as trustees.

One of the definitions of a human rights activist is a good law-and-order citizen who has been wrongfully arrested. Marilyn Brown (who I'll discuss later) was a perfect example. So was my first chairman, Col. Derek Sherrard- Smith, Royal Signals, who on his retirement had entered local politics as a Conservative and had been chairman of Surrey County Council. Earlier in the year his son, Gavin, after a secret trial in a religious court, had been flogged in Qatar, receiving fifty lashes for selling drink to a Muslim policeman. The British Government's efforts to prevent the flogging were undermined by public support from Terry Dicks, a Tory MP and chair of Friends of Qatar. He was even understood to have telephoned the ruler of Qatar to voice his support for the punishment.

I could not have wished for a wiser chair of trustees. Derek was already seventy-two when he agreed to help and only gave up five years later, when he felt he could no longer travel from his home in Surrey to my home where we held our trustee meetings.

In the summer of 1995, having got rid of Phil, the trustees found themselves with a spare salary and for the first time we were in a position to find someone who could help me on the professional side. We were resolved not to continue to run an office for case-work. There was only £20,000 a year to spend and we could not afford a full-time, qualified lawyer to take charge of it. I would have to do with someone who had legal training and could work from their own home until we could put our funding on a better footing. With grants came a need for double-entry bookkeeping. I came to an arrangement with John Ford, the Irish accountant who looked after the books of my old solicitor's firm, and he worked part-time for us. John was a sheer delight to work with. His Irish wit kept us cheerful through some very gloomy staff meetings. A middle-aged bachelor, his heart was in a property he had bought in Spain, which he was generous enough to allow our staff to use for holidays when he was not there.

Maitre Robert Thompson was the first foreign lawyer to contact me on the launching of fair trials. He was a living example of *entente cordiale*. Born of Anglo-French parentage, he held dual nationality and after qualifying as a solicitor in England worked in Europe during the 1950s. He then settled down in private practice in Dover, acting as honorary Consul for France. At some time before I met him he had relocated to France and by the 1990s was the honorary Consul for the United Kingdom in Boulogne. Completely bilingual, but already in his late sixties and bent double by spine disease, he was my best guide to the French justice system and a great representative in court. For that first year I put him on a modest retainer. He combined his practice in the Pas-de-Calais with representation on behalf of truckers with the French judicial authorities.

Together we explored the bizarre way of handling interstate evidence at the time. A British trucker with a home in Kent had been arrested in Calais and, represented by Robert, appeared before a local examining magistrate. The examining magistrate adjourned the hearing for enquiries into the possibility of a British criminal record. Such enquiries had to go on a circuitous journey. The official request would wend its way up to the appropriate department in the Ministry of Justice in Paris, officially translated into English, sent over to the appropriate department in the British Home Office and down to the local police (never mind Kent being twenty-two miles away from Calais). After about four months the examining magistrate, having heard nothing and concerned at the lack of progress, asked Robert if he could make informal enquiries. Robert and I chased the request through the French and British systems and back came the cryptic report 'known to the police'. The magistrate was somewhat puzzled. 'I am known to the police, so what?' He sent Robert off to make further enquiries. Months passed with our poor client on remand in Longueville. Eventually an official response arrived. The prisoner was only known to the Kent police because of the first enquiry from the magistrate!

Over the next couple of years I managed to evolve a way of coping with staff against our background of chronically unreliable funding and the virtual office. My management style was eccentric and probably totally unsuitable for a commercial organisation. We didn't have a hierarchy. Staff were hired to deal with specific projects, the project money was usually for one year and therefore the standard contract of employment was for one year with the understanding that if we could get the project money renewed, the contract would be renewed as well. Everyone worked from home and management control, such as it was, consisted of lengthy telephone calls, face-to-face meetings in central London where necessary, usually at the Law Society, and monthly staff meetings. I needed – and found – gifted and talented people who enjoyed the independence I was able to give them. They would come to me if they were troubled or had made a mistake but would not fret despite often being out of their depth.

It must have been unusual to face my standard question at the job interview. 'I'm out of the country on a mission. The telephone lines have been switched to you. A story on one of our cases has broken. *Newsnight* is on the line. Jeremy Paxman wants you to take part in the discussion. Could you cope?' All my long-term, operational staff actually had to face this sort of situation when the rest of us were away.

Our staff meetings were three-line-whip affairs and held at lunchtime on the canteen floor of the Royal Festival Hall. It was important that someone arrived early and secured a table and chairs as far away from the lunchtime concert as possible. The competition was intense. There were usually a dozen other business meetings taking place around us.

What I had going for me was the nature of the cause and the commitment of everyone associated with it. While commercial organisations would be plagued with people taking sickies, it was quite an important function of mine at the monthly meetings to note whether anybody looked exhausted or unwell and order them to take a break. A number of people came and went, but I was fortunate enough to acquire a couple of other long-term colleagues over this period.

Patricia Reccio Ferrer – known as Patri – was looking for employment in this country because her partner was British and studying for a doctorate. Although she was only in her early twenties she had serious high-flying credentials, having just completed a stint as senior assistant to a Spanish MEP. She was not legally trained, but her European and Spanish connections were to prove extremely useful to us and she often came abroad with me. She had the title of European Development Officer and was basically funded by a grant from Europe to compile a databank of European lawyers who would act for foreigners in their native country.

I always regarded Patri as a senior colleague. She was extremely shrewd and mature, although at first glance she could be taken for a young secretary. She became a secret weapon in an important series of interviews for a research job we jointly sponsored with Warwick University. The interviewees were not to know that the charming receptionist who chatted to them whilst they waited to be inter-viewed was in fact a member of the selection panel. Her succinct character assessments prevented us from making a serious mistake. She also had to take the *Newsnight* practical whilst I was out of the country.

I was visiting Madrid with Patri to lobby the Spanish Presidency on the need for international procedural reform within the European Union. She had managed to get me an interview with the top civil servant in the Ministry of Justice. When I tried to press the case for the establishment of the proper legal aid system in Spain, I was met with the comment: 'What's the point of wasting money? They're all guilty!'

In the late 1990s I fitted in a visit to one of Madrid's main prisons to meet a middle-aged, West Country hotelier who had been arrested on a charge of conspiracy to smuggle drugs into Spain. He had been preparing to retire to southern Spain and thought he would find out whether it was worthwhile taking up an agency to import agricultural machinery from the West Country, where he had good connections, to the area where he wanted to settle. He went to Spain, advertised in the local English-speaking newspaper and received a telephone call inviting him to a meeting with a prospective customer in his Spanish hotel bar. It turned out that the 'prospective customer' was part of a drug ring and under surveillance by the police. On the evidence of the unrecorded meeting he had been arrested and convicted.

I visited him in Modulo prison. On the other side of the ubiquitous chicken-wire grille stood an unkempt, unshaven man who appeared to be in his sixties. He started by making what I took to be masonic signs and asking me whether I was on 'the square'. I have little experience of masons. He then said he was innocent and burst into tears. It was the only experience I have actually had of a grown man in obvious distress and it made an abiding impression on me. Despite all our usual appeals to both governments they fell on deaf ears and we did not manage to help him.

I was so sad when personal problems forced Patri and her partner to relocate to Madrid after a couple of years. We did manage to get her grant renewed and she continued to work with us from our Madrid 'office', which was her flat. She proved even more useful as our Spanish representative and was quite outstanding as a paralegal. In one case, of her own initiative, she sought an audience with a Spanish examining magistrate and persuaded him that under the International Law on Human Rights he had no business continuing to hold our client. He was freed. Eventually the grants supporting her salary came to an end and we had to part company.

Through the evidence discussed later in the Campaign for European Justice, I clearly needed expert advice on the training of court interpreters. I discovered that a Home Office sponsored Nuffield project existed and consulted its coordinator, Sarah de Mas, because it was obvious Europe needed something similar. We met a second time and I offered her the job of coordinating a European project that she would design. She accepted, and it was then I mentioned that it was subject to her joining me on a visit to Brussels to get funding. It was as well she had a great sense of humour.

Sarah was an intellectual Mother Courage. Left a widow in her mid-twenties with two young children to raise, she put herself through Cambridge and obtained a qualification in business management from Leicester University. When I met her she was in her forties. We managed to get her two years of funding for the European Legal Interpreters Project: a pilot survey of the qualifications required in five European countries. By the end of the two years she was indispensable. She had become my junior partner and we would take joint decisions on most matters. There was one nasty year where we missed out on the funding and I was forced to carry her salary from my personal resources but she remained with me as my deputy until my retirement in 2006.

I think our relationship was best expressed as creative tension. Coolly analytical and organised, she was the perfect foil to my chaotic way of working. It was she who persuaded me that flying by the seat of my pants was no longer tenable and we really needed an aircraft. With her background of academia and charity we quarrelled over such things as the necessity of footnotes to our positional papers and the primacy of professional ethics (client confidentiality) over Charity Commissioners' demands for case details. On the other hand our positional papers got better and better as we learned how to collaborate on them.

One of the problems in receiving grants from Brussels was the official inspection during the course of the grant. Representatives of the European Commission would come on a mission of inspection to the UK and over the course of a week hold meetings with the recipients of grants and inspect the accounts. The first year I received notice of the visitation with some consternation. I could just see the impression we would make in the Festival Hall. Word came through that they would only have time to meet us between three and six on a weekday afternoon. It was Patri who suggested the solution. We booked a large table at The Ritz in Piccadilly for their traditional afternoon tea and in the civilised atmosphere of this iconic hotel we met the two-member delegation over thin cucumber sandwiches to the strains of the Palm Court Orchestra. 'You're so European,' exclaimed the Italian, as I introduced her to my Irish accountant and Spanish and German colleagues. We got a good report and word must have got around about the London-based eccentrics who worked without an office to save money. I entertained future delegations round my kitchen table in the evenings when they made an overnight stop in Richmond.

The primitive briefing paper on cross-border injustices in Europe was in demand in the UK. Throughout the first eighteen months of FTA, I found myself briefing an increasing number of Members of Parliament from all parties who were dissatisfied with the lack of Consular support for their innocent constituents. By the end of 1994 I could count on more than twenty such supporters, amongst them the charismatic Mo Mowlam, who later became the Secretary of State responsible for creating the Good Friday agreement in Northern Ireland. She had two current cases at the time and she suggested that we form a Justice Group in the House of Commons. She then circulated all the MPs who had already contacted me. In January 1995 we held a preliminary meeting in a House of Commons committee room. The meeting was a fiasco. There had been a change of venue and half the MPs turned up at the old committee room. They decided to meet formally in March.

Between the two meetings Mo Mowlam obtained a frontbench position and had to drop out. The MPs who turned up at the second meeting, to which I was not invited, elected Dr Robert Spink as the chairman. Dr Spink was in Parliamentary terms an extreme right-winger, who for a short period joined the United Kingdom Independence Party (UKIP) and became its only sitting MP. The group struggled on for a meeting or two and then fizzled out. We made efforts over the years to see if there was a possibility of resurrecting the group but nothing ever came of them. The problem with busy Members of Parliament was that they were only interested in the topic if they had a constituent who qualified for support, and then only as long as the constituent's problems persisted. This made for a constant churning of active members of Parliament and by 1996 the whole topic had been subsumed into the all-party Parliamentary Human Rights Committee.

I had still not solved the problem of being the sole professional.

Though both Patri and Sarah were extremely good paralegals, perfectly capable of doing casework under supervision, I had no one around me who could both read the files and take decisions on them. But I could leave the commonsensical Sarah to look after FTA when I took holidays or was away on missions abroad.

The events that transformed our status within the European Union started with the UK European Parliamentary elections of June 1999. The previous European Parliamentary elections of 1994 had been held with large constituencies under the traditional British 'first past the post' system. Only two Liberal Democrats had been elected to the Parliament. Both of them sat for the Devon and Cornish constituency – which includes Gibraltar! One of them was Graham Watson, an old acquaintance from the days when he had been an assistant to David Steel. He been a supporter of FTA from the beginning but otherwise we'd had little to do with each other since his specialisation was European finance. By June 1999 the voting system had been changed to proportional representation. Eleven Liberal Democrats were returned with Graham as leader, which constituted the largest national block of Liberals in the Parliament. Graham had become an important player.

Towards the end of July, Graham telephoned me to say he had just been selected as chair of one of our two key committees, the Civil Liberties committee. He was extremely keen on the topic of defendants' rights within the European Union, but had no detailed knowledge and needed a thorough briefing before the Parliament reconvened the following month. Could I meet him at the European Parliament offices as soon as his Italian holiday had finished? We made an appointment even though it meant cutting short our own holiday. I nearly drowned getting there.

7

'Game Changer' (1999–2000)

Minden Rose is much more than a thirty-two foot long keel Vancouver sailing yacht. Together with her predecessor, a twenty-seven foot Vancouver called Moon Billy, she has been our second home and a refuge from our hectic suburban lives since the early 1980s. August would normally have been the time for our usual West Country cruise. We generally sailed westward from our home base in the quintessentially English sailing town of Lymington in Hampshire. We would sail down the coast to Devon and Cornwall and, with a good weather umbrella, as far as the Scilly Isles before turning back. This year had to be different. Clearly the meeting with Graham Watson on the morning of Monday, 15th August was vital. I just had to be home by the evening before.

On the morning of 13th August we were in Cornwall. I listened to the weather reports at 5.30am and decided to leave at once. Strong easterly winds (blowing against us) were forecast for 'later', which in sailing terms means more than twelve hours away. By teatime, we had completed those twelve hours and were pretty tired, so we dropped into Brixham for a shower and a quick bite to eat. It was the end of the regatta, firework night. As we started to cross Lyme Bay we were treated to a great display. All the time the wind was rising, the sea was getting rougher, and using the engine alone was getting extremely uncomfortable. Sally persuaded me to try a scrap of sail. The motion of the boat got easier but there was no way I could hold a north-easterly course against a north-easterly gale. We were approaching Portland Bill, the most treacherous headland on the south coast. The pilot books recommend keeping at least twelve miles south of it in these conditions. No problem, I thought. I was heading unsteadily south-east and we had sailed off all our charts in the general direction of Cherbourg. I think it was 2am when Sally decided she needed to go to the heads (sailor's term for loo).

'Come quick, there's an awful lot of water down here and every time we hit a wave it's coming through the floorboards!' she called out to me. I put on the autopilot and dashed down to see what was going on. We couldn't find any obvious hole and the water was still rising. It was a Micawber situation. If the water could be pumped out faster than it was coming in, result happiness and safe harbour in Lymington. If the water was going to come in faster than it could be pumped out, result misery, distress rockets, S.O.S and abandon ship. After about an hour, taking it in turns to man the bilge pump, we were winning. Dawn broke on the morning of 14th August, the wind moderated and we headed north back onto our charts. The GPS revealed we were well on course and approaching Christchurch Bay. A lifeboat hurtling in the opposite direction slowed down long enough to tell us there was a strong wind warning. Too kind! We arrived at our berth in Lymington Marina exhausted and hungry, but alive. The following morning I made it to the European Parliament building in time for the crucial meeting with Graham Watson.

The European Parliament office gave every appearance of being deserted. It took some time to rouse the caretaker, though he did confirm that that there was one booking made for that day by Graham Watson. There were dust sheets over the furniture, building work going on everywhere and the noise of drilling on the upper floors. The caretaker found a committee room for us in the basement and Graham arrived shortly afterwards. We went through my briefing document and he said he was going to discuss it with the Secretary to the Civil Liberties Committee later that week.

The meeting turned out to be the start of 'the year of the game changer'. In August 1999, FTA was an NGO in financial crisis doing good work, without much real influence on either the national or European stage. Although I had made regular journeys to Brussels for several years, and always attended the old Civil Liberties subcommittee, as it then was, I was never invited to speak since it concentrated on other matters, and the chair, a Dutch liberal, was somewhat right-wing and more interested in police powers. Within twelve months FTA was an established charity with a secure financial base advising governments and international institutions.

In October I received a letter from the Charity Commissioners granting us charitable status at last. It had been more than four years since I first discussed with Andrew the possibility of becoming a charity. We knew it was always going to be a fight, but I suppose two years or so had been wasted through the poisonous intervention of the Foreign Office. There were modifications of our trust deed and other minor matters that would need sorting out at our next trustees meeting, but at last we could begin attempting to raise money from the major British sources of charitable funding.

November was an incredibly busy month. I'd had to attend two conferences in Brussels in consecutive weeks. One had been organised by the Civil Liberties committee of Parliament, where I spoke, and the second conference was about the new Charter of Fundamental Freedoms. Whilst I had grave reservations about a voluntary charter, which everybody would disregard, it was necessary to get it right in the hope that one day it might become compulsory.

With the help of Sarah, we had prepared and revised four positional papers: observations on the Tampere summit (in Finland in 1999); the Charter of Fundamental Freedoms; the scoreboard for progress on the Tampere programme (scoreboards were in vogue at the time, rather as roadmaps are now: a tick-box way of monitoring progress without the effort and cost required of setting up an independent agency); and the structure of the Commission for Justice and Home Affairs. It was the last paper that proved to be the only one of any long-term consequence for justice in the EU. At the time there was a law enforcement task force in the Justice and Home Affairs Commission, but nothing for civil liberties. We proposed a task force for Civil Liberties as well as the law-enforcement task force with two different lines of funding, one for each task force. The suggestion was not entirely disinterested – we thought a

Civil Liberties line of funding would make it easier for us to get money.

The trustees meeting at the end of that year, 1999, was a changeover meeting. It proved to be the last meeting chaired by Derek Sherrard Smith; Christopher Bayne, one of my friends who lived in the next village whom I persuaded to become a trustee, took over and chaired for the next six years. It was the first meeting for Peter Lipscomb, OBE, my next-door neighbour. From the beginning he was a source of strength and sage advice. Eventually he was to take over the chairmanship of FTA in the crisis after I retired and propelled the FTA forward to its current position. It was also the first meeting for Hans Warendorf, our first European trustee and our financial saviour in the years to come. Another newcomer was Belinda Harding, my cousin by marriage, who was to prove the contrarian that every organisation needs. She tested out all our bright ideas. It was the first meeting of the team of trustees who were to provide leadership for the next seven years.

I spent much of the year, often with Sarah, going backwards and forwards from Brussels to brief and advise both Parliamentarians and members of the Commission. The European Parliament works on lunar cycle. The first week is generally spent in discussion with national political groups, the second week in the European political groupings, the third week in Parliamentary committee meetings and for the fourth week everyone decamps to Strasbourg for the plenary sessions. So far as we were concerned, the key meetings were the committee meetings. We arrived for the two days of activities surrounding the meetings of the Civil Liberties Committee, to give us time not only to discuss matters with the MEPs on the Committee but to contact all the behind-the-scenes 'fixers' who guided the work of the Committee and sorted the agenda. The groups we relied upon for influence on the Committee were the Liberals, the Greens and Socialists. Between them they had a majority during that Parliament.

In May, Alan Davies (see Foreign Office Relations) was due to spend his sixtieth birthday in the Bangkok Hilton. Long-running cases tend to be forgotten by the media and the public unless there are specific events attached to them, such as a trial or an appeal pending. Father's Day, Mother's Day – why not Victim's Day to shine the spotlight on John's case, and whilst we were about it, three or four other ones? We chose the third Thursday in May and the format was such a success that it was continued annually throughout my watch. The original package for each client was their Member of Parliament and at least one relative. We got one of the MPs to book a committee room in the House of Commons, so that we could rely on the Parliamentary press corps to attend, and we usually had the Westminster reporters for regional television there as well. Alan Davies and Steve Bryant were represented. Other clients were lorry driver Richard Hudson in Macedonia and Rachel McGee in Cuba.

Richard Hudson transported goods for NATO to Skopje. There was a trumped-up involvement in a road accident where a Macedonian and a Serb were killed. He had not actually been in the collision. The car carrying the Macedonian and the Serb had lost control, skidded and hit another lorry behind. The expert report on the incident estimated the speed of the car at approximately 130 km/h (80 mph). Our investigation discovered a build-up of public resentment against NATO drivers in Macedonia caused by the protection of previous drivers in a series of fatal accidents involving natives. Ten locals had been killed in three previous incidents and those responsible were all extricated by NATO or their own governments. Richard Hudson was abandoned by the FCO on the orders of the Ministry of Defence and left to his fate.

Rachel McGee had been arrested by the Cuban authorities on drug charges in November 1998. An acquaintance, Remy, had offered her a cheap air ticket to join him for a fortnight's holiday in Cuba. The party eventually consisted of two couples. The other couple, Desmond Gordon and his girlfriend Michelle Malcolm were introduced by Remy in Cuba. At the time of her arrest, Rachel and Remy had gone to the hotel where Desmond and Michelle were staying. Remy told her to go away since he had boring business to discuss. She had started to leave and got into a taxi when she heard a row going on in the hotel. The police had pounced on her friends for drug smuggling, though no drugs were ever produced, and she returned to see what she could do and was rounded up with the others. At their trial, which occurred the following September, she was told not to give evidence, despite her protests, by the state-appointed lawyer who represented all of them. She received a sentence of fifteen years... An appeal was entered by the lawyer and lost. All the others were known to law enforcement authorities but Rachel had a clean record and was in employment. At no stage had anyone even bothered to take a statement from her.

Her mother came to see me after the appeal was over. It was clear to me that something was wrong. Everyone else was Jamaican. If there had been an Irish gang arrested for arms smuggling and there had been an Afro-Caribbean picked up with them, someone would have asked some questions, so why not the other way around? Rachel's mother had got her daughter to write a detailed statement of what had happened to her – forty pages of paper, the whole lot written in capital letters without a single punctuation mark from start to finish. Sally and I spent the best part of a week of evenings puzzling it out and rewriting it. I sent the revision to the Foreign Office. Luckily Baroness Scotland was due to make a ministerial visit to Fidel Castro. We created a lot of publicity about the state of the law and how dependent we were on Fidel Castro to be magnanimous to this poor Irish, working-class girl. She and the other female member of the party were both released a couple of months after Victim's Day, though no admissions were ever made. The Cubans announced shortly afterwards that the single-firm monopoly for defending foreigners had ended and two more sets of lawyers were going to be allowed to represent them.

In the middle of the year we were struck by financial disaster. Funding had been underpinned by an EU grant from the Secretary General's fund, which was our main core funding. We had to rely on my personal guarantee for the overdraft, most of the EU money being paid in arrears. But, provided I didn't take a salary, we eventually caught up. This time the fund administrator told me that he had run out of money for us. The entire fund had been pre-empted by European Parliament resolutions leaving his department with nothing to give. I went to Brussels in July to see whether anything could be done and had no luck. How could we survive?

The next morning I caught the first Eurostar train out of Brussels feeling very depressed. As I saw it, arrears of core funding would be coming in over the next year but we were likely to be fifty per cent short. It was a stark choice. Unless I was actually willing to keep the overdraft going and, in the last resort, find about £50,000, I couldn't keep Sarah and would have to manage without staff. It would amount to going back to where I began but ten years older and not in the best of health.

Still, I was looking forward to an interesting break on the journey home. Archie Kirkwood, the Scottish Liberal Democrat MP, had a lorry driver constituent of his who had been convicted of drug smuggling in France and was imprisoned in Longueville, the major prison for foreign convicts in north-east France. In June, he decided to go to visit his constituent and made arrangements through our local Consul for permission to visit. He was anxious for me to join him but there was no funding for my expenses. The plan was that I would stop off at Lille, near the prison; he would meet me at the station. He would pay for the taxi and we would travel to London together on a later train. He greeted me with the news that there had been a cock-up in getting his visit permit. I couldn't see the prison authorities refusing permission for a MPs visit to his constituent, so we went to the prison.

The warden of the main gate called the head warden, who explained that it was a public holiday, which we had quite forgotten, and he was 'desolate' but the distinguished foreign Parliamentarian and the legal representative could not be permitted to enter the prison without the magistrate's permission, and since she was on holiday and could not be disturbed, that was that.

I'd been hearing a lot of excited chatter coming from a large hall next door. What was that about?

'Ah, sir, that is quite different. On our public holidays, of course, family visits are always allowed.' There was a pause. 'Come to think of it, how fortunate it is that our Scottish prisoner is being visited by a couple of his elderly uncles today.'

So Gaelic independence and practicality defeated bureaucracy and we got a family visit. It was probably held under better conditions than if we'd been allowed in as normal. As we got into the taxi for our return journey to Lille I couldn't help laughing.

'What's up?' asked Archie.

'There's nothing like celebrating Bastille Day in traditional style,' I replied. 'Storming a French prison...'

On the way home, Archie expressed an interest in our work and I told him how worried I was about finances. It turned out he was chairman of the Joseph Rowntree Reform Trust, one of the great Quaker charitable funders, with an interest in penal reform. He asked me to send him our appeals letter and the budget as soon as possible. A month or two later a cheque for £45,000 arrived in the post. It was going to be enough to tide us over for the year.

'Toby' Keith Bromley was already well over eighty when I met him at a prison reform meeting. A member of the Russell & Bromley shoe family, he knew my father through their mutual interest in breeding Aberdeen Angus cattle. In 1989, Toby had set up the Bromley Trust which he termed 'the most important work of my life' committed to 'offset man's inhumanity to man'. He endowed the Bromley Trust with much of his fortune.

We were extremely grateful when in 2000 his trust sent us a couple of thousand pounds and followed with similar relatively small sums for the next couple of years. I then received a telephone call from Teresa Elwes, who explained that she was Keith's niece and had taken over the running of the trust. She wanted to meet all recipients of grants at their offices. She explained that since she was working as a full-time forensic pathologist, she was somewhat restricted in date and time, but still wanted come and see me at my 'offices' in Richmond. I was very nervous at the thought of a scientific young professional coming to meet me in my shambles of a study to discuss what I was doing. I could only imagine the businesslike approach of the other charities the trust supported. We were probably due for dissection.

When she arrived she didn't have much time, but I got the impression she was a very competent and organised person. As she left, I thought 'There goes our grant'. I was quite astonished to receive a telephone call from her explaining how impressed she was with our work and that she would be recommending to the trustees that not only should we receive the maximum grant they allowed, £10,000 a year, but we could count on their continued support. From that day to this, we have always received a grant from the Bromley Trust.

That autumn, Sarah and I went to Brussels to attend a meeting of the Civil Liberties Committee. The last appointment before the Committee was due to sit was with Anna Tyrone, leader of the Socialists. We talked about the problem of the preferred list for grants. Anna told us that it was on the agenda that morning. She would try and put us on it.

About half an hour later, the grants were discussed and Anna proposed our inclusion. The motion was put to a vote; all members turned towards their group leaders. The Liberal and Green hands shot up to join the Socialists. We never had any trouble with being allotted a grant again. The *annus mirabilis* ended, thanks to Sarah, with the help I had desperately needed ever since the beginning: the Nuffield Foundation had awarded us a three-year grant to pay for a legal caseworker.

8

'Hot Desk' (2000–2003)

The search for a legal caseworker began with a postage-stamp sized advertisement in *The Guardian*, complete with minuscule logo. It was very expensive. It was a surprise that *The Guardian*, itself a trust, should charge small charities large sums to advertise. We made huge demands in the advert. Applicants had to be EU citizens, qualified lawyers and speak both English and either French or German to 'mother tongue standard'. This was the politically and legally correct way of saying that only French, German or dual nationals were being considered. We needed to balance our team for Europe.

We were overwhelmed with applicants, about half of them considering GCSE French grades to be mother tongue standard, and quite a few of the rest deciding their third-class law degrees would do as qualification. We were a bit surprised, despite all this, to get six serious candidates worth interviewing.

Sarah and I decided to interview the three best candidates on paper, with a reserve list. Two candidates proved to be quite outstanding. In fact, we couldn't separate them at first interview, invited them back with Peter Lipscomb joining the panel for the second interview and still couldn't make up our minds. Both were women. The younger of the two had been qualified as a German lawyer for the past couple of years and also held a higher degree from the London School of Economics, where she had specialised in Human Rights Law. During her legal training she had worked with the German mission to the UN in New York, with a French law firm in Paris and acted as a trainee prosecutor at the Hamburg Juvenile

71

Court. After qualifying she worked as a lawyer for the Civil Liberties Committee of the European Parliament. Wow!

The other one, Sabine Zanker, also German, was considerably older and had much more practical experience as a defence lawyer in Germany. As an elected member of the Council of her hometown of Tübingen she had served as deputy Mayor for five years. The integration of ethnic and social minorities into the community, with a particular emphasis on human rights for refugees, was at the centre of her political commitment.

In the end we offered them a job share, which suited them both. The younger one wanted to complete a research degree and Sabine was busy settling her five children and academic husband into England from Australia.

I was not too surprised when the younger one left us for a more exciting job, but Sabine Zanker stayed with us. My abiding memory of her, even from the beginning, was her extraordinary competence and a Germanic eye for detail. This worked beautifully alongside my own 'key issue' approach to casework. She was a true solicitor in her humanity – so much so that there was the occasional grumble that she was devoting too much time to social work, as opposed to legal work, for some of the clients. I had hoped that she would put herself forward as my successor but she decided that her work/life balance would be thrown out of kilter with the demands of being chief executive. I can never recall having a cross word with her although I knew by her silence when she disapproved of something that I thought was a good idea.

Quite early on in our relationship, she proved how important it was to have a good professional caseworker assisting me. The background work in the plane spotters' case involved taking statements, liaising with the Greek lawyer as well as acting as backup for me, both in the UK and Greece. It would have been impossible to complete the other urgent legal and advisory work I was involved in, had it not been for her.

It was Sabine who changed our lifestyle. She was the first senior who did not want to work from home. She needed an office. It was something she was used to and she wanted a measure of separation between home and work. It was clearly going to be important with two caseworkers to have the files accessible centrally. We also needed conference rooms, places to meet clients and hold our own Trustee and staff meetings. My home, meetings in The Law Society's public rooms and our old fallback, the Festival Hall, spoke volumes for our enthusiasm, but did little to convey professionalism. I think it was Sarah who discovered a charitable floor in a neo-modern office block over Waterloo station. Although there were plans to pull it down in the near future it would give us some years of centralised services. The charitable floor paid no rates and was virtually open plan. 'Hot desks', with a corresponding floor area, were hired at something like £4,000 per annum, which included all services and a booking system for the conference rooms. We could only afford two desks and three chairs but it meant that Sabine had an office of sorts and we all had a central meeting place. After a couple of years the offices were redeveloped, but we found another charitable floor let on the same basis at Number One, London Bridge, where we stayed for the rest of my time.

Those of us who are humanists do not think much about our own demise and its consequences until things start to go wrong. In 1999, I began to slow down, and felt physically exhausted. I thought it just a consequence of being in my mid-sixties. After all, I had run a marathon only a few years before.

When we start our summer cruise, we always anchor in Studland Bay, just outside Poole in Dorset, for a day or two. It is our custom to go ashore the morning after we arrive and walk uphill for about a mile to a viewpoint opposite a famous rock, old Harry. That year, I was not only slow, I couldn't make it. We had a serious discussion in which Sally told me she had noticed my jogging was slowing down to such an extent she could walk quicker than I could move. I had to promise to go to our GP for a check-up. I was referred to a cardiologist.

In October 1999, at Kingston Hospital, I was wired to an ECG and put on a running machine that gradually got faster. About halfway through the circuit I began to feel so rotten I stopped. The supervisor looked at the printout and rushed out of the room to fetch the cardiologist. He started to take my pulse in all my limbs, without any explanation. I was quite terrified I'd done something awful to myself.

He left me with the remark that no permanent damage had been done and mentioned casually, 'By the way, have you had angina long? Anyway, we will need to do something. The cardiology nurse will see you shortly if you wait outside.'

I don't know how long I had to wait – probably only a few minutes. I knew nothing about heart trouble and my close relatives had all lived to a ripe old age. My mother was getting on for ninety. My father died at ninety-six. 'Angina' was something one got when one needed a quadruple bypass – and I hadn't made a will. The extremely pleasant specialist nurse eventually came and calmed me down but there was nothing really to worry about. I hadn't had a heart attack as I'd feared, but I might have some minor artery trouble. They could look around nowadays inside the heart and fix such trifles by passing a tube through a vein in the thigh. I needed to spend only one night in hospital. I had an angioplasty the following month.

The next year I had an enormous fever and remained in hospital. Doctors diagnosed some type of heart virus and had great fun using search patterns with combinations of antibiotics until they found one that worked several days later. Chronic bed shortages meant being placed in the geriatric ward for stroke patients. I not only lowered the average age by several years, it meant being the only able-bodied person there who could ring for a nurse and I spent most disturbed nights pressing my buzzer to bring a nurse to some other patient.

By 2002, it was discovered I needed a pacemaker. Then other things went wrong. I began to suffer from '3pm syndrome'. A classic occurred: dreaming of chairing an FTA staff meeting, I woke up to find it to be true. Meeting-packed trips abroad were stressful at the best of times but by the sixth or seventh meeting of the day I had lost the plot and noticed people politely asking me to go over what I'd said since they didn't quite grasp the point. As a precaution, I began to take Sarah with me on all these trips. She observed one meeting in Spain where I started talking rubbish, which deeply shocked her.

The combination of stress and age took its toll. Small charities are not businesses. In business, if your work is in demand the turnover increases, more money comes in and you can afford to hire extra staff and make your job less demanding as you age. FTA at this stage was a greater demand than ever. About then I learned that over two thirds of small charities did not survive the death or incapacity of the founder in harness. I took no salary but my successor would need one, so in the summer of 2003 I gave my trustees three years notice so we could find the money. The end of my watch hove into sight.

9

Staggering Towards Retirement (2003 to 2006)

I had begun the process of planning for retirement in the summer of 2002 by drafting a five-year plan and presenting it to the trustees. It began: *'Very recently, due to a combination of the European parliament civil liberties committee resolution. . . and committee control of funding. . . we shall receive a substantial part of our funding as permanent core funding for our work in Europe year on year. What this means to us is that we have a financial basis for entering into realistic strategic planning. We would need a new chairman and also a new director sometime within the next five years.'*

I tried to produce a broad-brushstroke forecast and personal view of what might be a sensible strategy to aim for in the next five years and I went through various topics:

Casework: *'Our strategy over the next five years (indeed perhaps the next decade) has already been agreed: from a base of almost exclusively British clients we wish to expand to cover all the other European nationalities. Since such indications we have are that the incidence of injustice to citizens in the absence of special factors is linked to ovall population (more Germans than Danes, but there are special factors for the Dutch) we should be expanding our casework 500% over time. . . The casework is likely to grow ever more complex and intense and the numbers will increase.'*

There were *'hopes that by the end of the period, the needs for casework within the European Union will diminish due to the creation of adequate protection for European citizens. . .'* Wild optimism!

'By the end of the period The European legal system created by the European legal space will be fully operational.' Even more wild optimism!

'Our experience in fundraising, short though it is, should persuade us that we are unlikely to feel comfortable with a budget target that exceeds £200k in real

terms and that a realistic figure for planning purposes is somewhere between £150–180K… Throughout this period we will be unable to fund more than three such people with ancillary staff (e.g. part time administrator.) At present we are assured of funding two with somewhat uncertain arrangements for the third.'

I concluded: *'We will continue to be a small organisation with big responsibilities and hopefully influence to match throughout this period. The priorities will continue to be casework on the one hand and ensuring a practical system of Justice for the citizen within the European Union on the other. The key to the survival and progress of FTA is its "troika": three talented people able to take absolute personal responsibility for their sectors and combine together as a team to react to major events and problems as they arise.'*

However, the real purpose of my paper was to get people to think about my retirement.

'I have taken advice from many outsiders on the perceived problem of arranging the retirement of a founder of a major organisation (the problem is not confined to NGOs or charities) that fundamentally needs "image" and political influence to obtain successful results for its mission.' I was still obsessed with the statistic that only one in three small charities survived the death or incapacity of a founder in office.

'Key factors: The retirement needs to be planned and a date to be set. The director needs to walk away from the job and become a passive Consultant: the new team needs to be responsible for the running of the organisation. I would like three more years earning money with a view to bolstering my pension arrangements.

We also need to give time for Sabine to gain experience and the easing of her personal domestic circumstances.

Trustees: current influx of trustees need time to familiarise themselves with the working of FTA. Change of chair (2005?) Should preferably not coincide with retirement of director.'

Financial: director should retire at end of a financial year.

Taking all these factors into account I think I would like to retire on 31st March, 2006. For others to consider: is seventy-one too old?'

Looking back on the paper I am struck by its unworldliness.

BBC Radio 4's week's *Good Cause* has its origins in the very first days of British public radio. There is enormous competition to get one of these slots, and we were lucky enough to be chosen as the good cause for the week at the end of January 2005. It is probably not generally realised that over the eighty years it has been running, a formula has developed. Once you have been selected, the producers of the series will take you in hand, advising you on what works and what does not. The script for the broadcast has to be exactly 400 words to fit into the time slot, and that includes the addresses to write to and the bank arrangements for direct contributions. What the listener hears on a Sunday evening is a finely crafted professional delivery. Charities are advised to get an actor or professional broadcaster to actually make the broadcast and we were lucky enough to have Jon Silverman, then the BBC's home correspondent, as a sympathiser, and it was he who delivered the broadcast. We built it around the plight of Marianne Telfer, a woman from Essex, whose Caribbean holiday had gone terribly wrong.

Only one item of news counted during the Christmas/New Year period before our broadcast: the terrible tsunami that devastated the shores around Indonesia and was responsible for the deaths of a large number of Britons on holiday in Thailand. January 2005 saw an enormous public drive by all major charities concerned with such disasters. In our myopic way we were concerned that all the week's *Good Causes* in the first two or three months of 2005 would be severely affected by compassion fatigue. In the event we raised the usual amount, somewhere between £5,000 and £10,000.

Dominican Republic: Marianne Telfer

Marianne's holiday had been spent at the most popular complex for foreign holidaymakers in the Caribbean: Puerto Plata in the Dominican Republic. On the final morning of the holiday – Monday, February 16th, 2004 – she returned from a last-minute shopping expedition to find her partner Richard having convulsions on the floor of their hotel room. They had a quarrel over calling the medical services and in the course of it he reluctantly admitted that he had been swallowing drugs in condoms to take back to Britain.

He soon had another fit and lapsed into unconsciousness. She telephoned the hotel management but by the time medical help arrived he had died. It transpired that some of the condoms he had swallowed had burst inside him and he had been poisoned by a massive overdose of cocaine.

The police immediately arrested Marianne and, despite a report from those in charge of the investigation clearing her of any involvement in Richard's drug-smuggling operation, she still sat, three months later, in Puerto Plata jail awaiting trial on serious drug charges that could have resulted in her incarceration for another ten years.

Such cases usually highlight serious defects in the justice system of the countries concerned. A common problem is the lack of competent legal assistance. In Marianne's case, we needed to find a suitable lawyer. I consulted various international criminal lawyers' associations, including our own European Criminal Lawyers' Advisory Panel (ECLAP), for the names of appropriate lawyers in the Dominican Republic. I could not get a practical recommendation and had to go on a mission, funded by the Telfer family with Sarah as interpreter, to find one.

We found a collection of criminal lawyers used to acting for professional drug couriers who could not conceive of an innocent client. One client a year would make them wealthy and all our contacts advised that the minimum charge for acting in drugs cases would be US$10,000 rising to as much as $25,000 (about ten years' income for many local lawyers.)

In order to keep expenses down, we went on a discounted 'holiday' for a week in the same holiday complex used by Marianne and her partner. I'd never been to the Caribbean before and it seemed a wonderful opportunity to give Sally a cheap holiday, so the three of us flew out together.

May 2004 saw day after day of sunshine and gentle coastal breeze. A mixture of electronically tagged (tags paid for all food and drinks)

British and German families led a morning rush from the apartments and flats surrounding the central swimming pool to park towels in the strategic deckchairs between pool and the bar. The Germans always won. There was similar 'Gadarene' behaviour to get first choice at the buffets, a sumptuous display of European and local cooking that gradually tailed off as the week passed. All around us was a colourful display of swimming costumes and flowered shirts.

Day after day I set out at the crack of dawn in my white shirt and smart grey trousers carrying a leather briefcase, with Sarah in a summer dress, returning as dusk approached. We consoled ourselves with the thought that the working week would end on the Friday and we were going to have a full weekend in the resort to enjoy ourselves. On Friday evening the tropical storm began. The rain wouldn't stop for four months!

The local British Consul had good connections. After a number of interviews with run-of-the-mill local lawyers we found Dr Oswaldo Echavarría, not only an excellent lawyer, but also married to the German Consul. He had European standards and agreed to take the case for a tenth of the local tariff.

Behind the scenes, I played politics. I had visited Marianne in the only place the area had for women prisoners, a section of a military prison. For the first and only time in my life, a guard gave me a full body search. They did the same to Marianne's father. Prison conditions were quite awful: no glass in the windows and the cell flooded in any rainstorm, mattresses soaked and mildew everywhere. Next door they had a brand new women's prison built to modern European standards with such luxuries as a computer training room for prisoners to learn IT skills. Prison officers had been sent to Spain for training. The Spaniards, as agents for the European Union, were responsible for this project, only one of many EU projects that underpinned the cost of the Dominican Republic justice system. The British lawyer interested no one, but an adviser to the European Union institutions had all doors open to him. They took me on a tour of the new prison, which opened whilst Marianne was still there. Finally I got an appointment with the State's attorney to the Dominican Republic who assured me that this regrettable incident would soon be sorted with an accelerated hearing of the appeal. It took a month or two, as these things do, but Marianne was acquitted and sent home.

In 2003, a retired distinguished diplomat – a relative of one of the trustees – considered joining the board. He approached his FCO contacts for guidance as to our reputation within the Foreign Office. He gathered, essentially, that I was the problem. In their eyes, my main faults were that 'I was too big for my boots, too close to my clients and too keen on the media'. My personal reaction at the time, apart from the need to buy bigger boots on the Nancy Sinatra principle, was they did me too much honour. They still had not learned that apart from ethical principles a solicitor is for all practical purposes his client, and the law of agency applies. It was a good thing that the media supported me. My unfortunate clients would have been, apart from hard-working constituency members of Parliament, otherwise friendless.

The downside was a belated recognition that the antagonism we were suffering from at the time was largely personal and, rightly or wrongly, I was part of the problem. For that reason alone, a change of leadership in FTA was necessary.

From the beginning of 2006, I pressed vigorously for the retirement and successor problem to be resolved. Like most trusts the officers – Christopher Bayne, the chair, and Peter Lipscomb – ran the business of the trustees between quarterly trustee meetings and we began discussions on succession problems. Despite our best endeavours, Christopher wished to retire. We faced the dilemma foreseen in the paper of 2002: simultaneous retirement of chairman and director. What we needed was a lawyer as either chair of trustees or chief executive.

We started the search for my successor against a background of growing hysteria and manoeuvring around the selection process Originally given the job of drawing up job specifications and drafting

81

an advertisement, at the next Trustees meeting they told me to get an outside agency to do this. The interviews took place without active staff participation. It made for a poisonous atmosphere in which none of the participants, including myself, came out with any credit.

In the end they chose an Australian chief executive. She was no lawyer, but she had an academic Human Rights degree, political experience and had successfully run a consumer rights NGO. Since she lived in Australia and we could not afford return fare and expenses, the trust appointed her on the basis of a series of conference phone interviews. I found her to be extremely personable when I eventually met her and she would have passed any face-to-face interview. On the other hand, we might have been able to probe into her future plans.

As she had to serve out three months notice in Australia, I staggered on as a lame duck chief executive. Staff meetings were really painful and some minor staff conflicts broke out into open warfare, resulting in the abrupt departure of one self-employed part timer.

Being caretaker gave me a personal dilemma during this stage. I couldn't make major changes, though at the very end Sarah and I managed to find premises with fellow legal rights organisation Justice as our landlords that allowed for expansion and proved very adequate for a number of years after we left.

At the time I really had had enough of running a sour organisation and couldn't wait for someone else to take over. I was suffering from burnout. At the next trustees meeting the chair announced I was to be 'founder and patron'. Active involvement ceased.

I watched in horror and despair as a very clean sweep was made. The incident that hurt me the most over this period, though there were a number of infantile squabbles, was the return of John Davies from Thailand in 2007. I'd put much time and energy into his case over the last decade. A moment's thought to tell me where and when he was arriving so I could be at the airport to greet him would have been normal courtesy. When we finally met up a month or two later he told me his first question at the airport had been 'Where's Stephen?' He couldn't understand why I wasn't there.

After just over a year, the new chief executive announced that she had found a new job which paid better. She gave short notice and left. Simultaneously, the new chair of trustees missed two successive trustee meetings, it was obvious she had to be replaced. The only stroke of luck to hit the organisation at that time was, since Peter Lipscomb, my cousin Belinda and Hans Warendorf had remained as trustees, Peter could take over the chair. He realised that the priority was to raise enough money to pay a proper lawyer to fill the role as chief executive and most importantly, to find a good one.

Jago Russell was a solicitor who had trained with a major city firm, then decided to leave the rat race and work with the human rights organisation Liberty. We were delighted when he agreed to become our new chief executive. Peter, my close friend and neighbour for over a decade, kept me in touch with developments.

Shortly afterwards, Jago and I found ourselves booked to attend the same Brussels experts' conference on pre-trial detention. On the first morning, we met in front of Jago's hotel and travelled together to the conference centre. I introduced him to the many familiar faces from NGOs and the commission who were attending the conference. I declined to speak but urged Jago to do so for FTA. He was an excellent speaker and as I watched his audience it was clear that FTA was back in Brussels after a painful absence. Together Peter and Jago shouldered the heavy task of repairing the neglected European links with legal practitioners and EU secretariat. After a couple of years it was obvious that FTA was entering a new level of both influence and support.

Part 3:
Case Book

10

Greeks

On November 8, 2001, an officially invited party of fourteen plane enthusiasts – twelve Britons and two Dutch nationals – were attending an air display at a Greek military airbase near Kalamata, when they were arrested, jailed and accused of espionage. They were held there for a month and eventually came to trial on April 25th, 2002. Found guilty on reduced charges, the sentences varied from twelve months to three years, all eventually suspended pending appeal, and they flew home on bail.

On Wednesday, May 1st, 2002, immediately after the original conviction, *The Times* published as their lead letter my account of what happened. Under the heading 'Doubtful justice for plane spotters' I wrote:

Sir

I was perhaps the only non-Greek lawyer present throughout the lamentable events last week in Kalamata. The prosecution case against the plane spotters consisted of an anonymous 'security statement' supported in evidence by a middle-ranking Greek air force officer. His evidence, such as it was, was hearsay. He consistently refused to answer any pertinent cross-examination points by the defence on the grounds either that he did not know or that they were matters of national security. The judges never pressed him to answer any of the questions he avoided. All the oral and written evidence given by three experts (one a Greek who testified to the existence of Greek plane spotters) and the plane spotters themselves was rejected in favour of a document of unknown provenance that couldn't be questioned.

You said (leading article, April 27) that 'it is rarely right that any government comment on the verdict reached after a fair trial' but this rests on the wholly unwarranted assumption that this trial was fair...

There has been much diplomatic talk about the Greek government being unable to intervene in judicial process. It all appears to be a smokescreen for what actually happened in this case. The standards of Greek judges are a responsibility of their Ministry of Justice and presumably the security services could have been ordered to desist by the government at any time.

A couple of days after the arrests, I had received a call from a relative of one of the prisoners and been given the telephone number of a Greek police station. He told me to ask for the wife of the tour organiser and the only woman in the party, Lesley Coppin. Telephone calls to foreign police stations are usually an exercise in patience. I dialled the number and braced myself for the inevitable delays and struggle to make myself understood before eventually – if ever – reaching Mrs Coppin. The call was picked up immediately. I said slowly, 'I am a British lawyer and I wish to speak to Mrs Lesley Coppin'.

'Speaking,' said Lesley. Apparently the Greek police station had been so inundated with phone calls from the UK that she had been 'promoted' to station telephone operator, none of the officers feeling confident enough to field the calls in English. It was a curtain raiser for my personal involvement in the tragi-comedy. This was a tragedy for the plane spotters, who suffered considerable financial hardship and mental distress in their year-long ordeal. However, by the time the first trial was over it was a farce, with clear touches of *Alice in Wonderland.* That telephone conversation was my introduction to our 'Alice'. Lesley, on her honeymoon with tour organiser Paul, was the only non-enthusiast. She had spent the entire incident at the airfield guarding the groups' cameras and doing crossword puzzles inside a locked van. It didn't stop her being arrested along with the rest.

The group eventually got bail after a month in Greek prisons. Lesley had the hardest time of it because she was separated from the others in a woman's prison. A Greek lawyer based in Athens with a British practice was in charge of the defence and our role in the UK was confined to obtaining witness statements. I met our lawyer in a

Marriott hotel on one of his frequent visits to London. His English was good and his confidence reassuring.

The group invited me to observe the trial at Kalamata, a town famous for its olives and not much else. Everyone shared the same hotel. Apart from the trial, the city seemed deserted. There was only one non-burger joint open for business in the evenings.

We'd arrived late the previous night and although tired, I couldn't sleep. I got up at 7am the day before the hearing and went for a stroll along the totally deserted beach. After about a quarter of an hour, I was about to turn around and head back for breakfast when I saw in the distance another figure trudging towards me, clearly also out for exercise. Surely English, but not one of the plane spotters. Must be a journalist.

'Good morning. Here for the trial?' I asked.

'Good morning. Yes,' he replied.

'Who do you represent? I'm the British lawyer.'

'Glad to meet you – I'm the editor of *Jane's Planes*. I'm supposed to be here as the plane spotters' expert witness, but you're the first person I have met.'

We turned back towards our hotel and discussed his evidence. We certainly spoke of many things. The Turkish right to instant access to any part of a Greek military airfield as a fellow member of NATO, Greek paranoia, plane spotting as a hobby in the United Kingdom and the Netherlands, Internet sites ...

I mentioned I hadn't had sight of his evidence. He told me that he'd just been told to turn up. I began to panic. Luckily, Greek working hours start early and I managed to raise one of our local lawyers to meet us for breakfast. I was right to panic. His statement had to be written, translated into Greek and lodged with the court and the prosecutor before the end of the working day. Our expert was led away and I did not see anything more of him until that evening when he told me they'd made the deadline.

I eventually recognised myself as the White Rabbit, constantly rushing from event to event looking at my watch. The problem was GMT – Greek Maybe Time. When someone in Greece tells you that the court will sit on Tuesday at 9am, it maybe Tuesday but certainly not 9am – maybe 10, maybe 11….. GMT drove British and Dutch journalists mad. On the eve of the first hearing, I was contacted by our Athens lawyer and told to arrange a press conference at seven o'clock. The television crews started setting up at about 6pm. I'd heard nothing more from Athens but felt sure our chief lawyer would be on his way. I arranged for our local lawyer to be on standby. By 7.15pm there was still no sign of our Athens lawyer and frantic attempts to reach him by phone yielded no results. We had to start the press conference without him. The local lawyer explained how the Greek law operated, while I commented on the international aspects of the case. We were into question time when I received a telephone call from the Big Man himself, informing me that all was well and he had just crossed the Corinth Canal – about two hours drive away!

Our Athens lawyer did not think much of the media. On the first day of the trial proper he told me during the lunch break that his Greek clients in London had sent him a barrage of complaints. They accused the BBC of criticising the Greek justice system and bringing the honour of Greece into disrepute. He thought it was also likely to hurt his practice if he did nothing about it. Would I join him in making an application to ban the BBC from the court for the rest of the trial? I told him I'd have nothing to do with it. It would do Greek reputation more harm than good to even suggest such a thing. To my surprise, he went ahead on his own and to my relief the application was thrown out.

The next morning, the trial started. Court proceedings start in Greece with a roll call of witnesses before the hearing can begin. The presiding judge was a diminutive woman of whom all the Greeks were clearly terrified. Definitely the Red Queen. She spoke in a shrill falsetto.

Even more impossible to ignore was the organisation of interpretation. There was only one Dutch interpreter for the two Dutch defendants. The fact that they had been directed to line up in alphabetical order meant that the two Dutchmen were separated and seated at either end of the row. How was the Dutch linguist to cope with that? There was also only one interpreter allocated to provide 'whisper' interpretation for all twelve British defendants. She would have had to shout. I managed to grab one of our lawyers. This trial could not go on until the seating was rearranged for the Dutch and we would need at least two more English interpreters. It took some time for me to get the message home to the lawyer and even more time for him to get the point across to the court. We adjourned for the day.

We did succeed in finding two extra interpreters, but contrary to international law we had to pay for them privately.

There were more adjournments over the next two days. We missed out one session due to a judge's strike for more pay. All these delays created a looming problem for the Greek judges: Greek Easter was approaching at the end of the week. They were quite determined to get rid of this case at any cost and not have it hanging over them during their holiday. By the time we actually started there were only two working days left. The result was a seventeen-hour marathon hearing lasting to the early hours of the following morning, with only a couple of meal breaks. Even the Greek lawyers had never heard of anything quite like this. It proved particularly difficult for me in my late sixties and the oldest person in the case. Despite my best efforts to keep awake, by 10pm I had completed a Dodgsonian metamorphosis from White Rabbit to Dormouse. Towards 2am the interpreters informed the court that they were too tired to carry on and the poor souls wanted to go to go home and get their heads down. Their application was refused. Worried Dutch and British Consular representatives nudged me awake, hauled me outside the courtroom and requested my expert opinion on whether the court had breached the European Convention on Human Rights. Suppressing the impulse to tell them that Article 3 – the one on torture – might apply, I told them that since all the rules on fair trial were designed to protect the accused, not anyone else involved, the interpreters had no remedy under international law. At their request, I took a poll of the plane spotters. They were quite as anxious as the judges to get it over with and so we carried on for nearly three more hours.

The only witness for the prosecution was the base security officer who had arranged the arrests. There was no whispering interpreter for me. Even so I could detect his repeated incantation in answer to questions posed by the defence. It sounded like a cross between an American witness pleading the Fifth Amendment and a Buddhist chant: a prisoner of war determined to stick to name, rank and number under all circumstances. At the start of the lunch break I gathered the litany was: 'I refuse to answer this question on the grounds that it might be a breach of national security'. He did, however, answer a few questions of little importance. When asked 'Why did the plane spotters attract your attention?' the reply was: 'It was their funny way of walking.' I did wonder where John Cleese got the idea from.

All the plane spotters were permitted to give evidence, which took up most of the evening. The highlight for me was Lesley Coppin's speech. She had been furious to learn she was not allowed to give evidence on oath. Our lawyers explained that this was a rule to stop people perjuring themselves in the witness box. Lesley made an impassioned plea that her love of all things Greek, especially Greek literature and theatre, made it quite impossible for her to do anything that might conceivably harm the Greeks and their State. She received a stony reception.

I heard all the evidence and had to go home at the final lunch break. If I'd missed the booked flight, the plane spotters would have had to club together to pay for a commercial flight and we couldn't see any point in paying extra. I gave a final interview to the British press just outside the court, and shared a hired taxi to Athens with our expert.

We spent Friday afternoon heading for Athens airport. At more than 2,000 metres up on a mountain pass in the central Peloponnese speeding round hairpin bends, a serious blizzard started, complete with thunder and lightning. Our driver had never stopped chatting on his mobile phone since we left Kalamata, clutching it to one ear whilst steering with the other hand. The storm obviously worried him, too. While he continued the chat, he grabbed a set of worry beads with the other hand, and steered with his knees. I looked at our expert: I think he had his eyes closed and murmured something. I closed my eyes too. I shall never know whether it was the God of my forefathers or Jesus Christ in his Protestant or Greek Orthodox manifestations that prevailed but somehow we did manage to get down that mountain.

When we finally arrived at Athens airport, I switched on my mobile. I was not surprised to find about forty messages waiting for me from journalists. I returned the first one to discover that the Red Queen had delivered a verdict amounting to 'Off with their heads!' I should have expected that. It was noticeable that the three judges never asked a single question of any of the witnesses during the case. The verdict had been decided upon before they started and they were just going through the motions. I should have also remembered that the Red Queen in the book had told Alice: 'Sentence first – verdict afterwards'. Only with great reluctance had 'Her Majesty' accepted our lawyer's plea to suspend sentences of immediate imprisonment pending appeal.

During the six months we had to wait for the appeal, I attended a crowded meeting with the then Foreign Secretary Jack Straw. In it he reminded everybody that he'd done everything he possibly could to support the plane spotters from the very beginning. Short of recalling our ambassador, the FCO *had* done everything they could. It was certainly the Greeks who were at fault.

Rumour had it the British and Dutch diplomatic services were getting tough. Information had been acquired from local sources that a top Greek judge had got tired of working within the Greek justice system and wanted to become a judge in either The Hague, or Strasburg. He needed international approval and word got to him that if the appeal went the right way, the appointment would receive official British and Dutch backing… On the other hand, if things went wrong he would be stuck in Athens!

Whatever the reason, the appeal in November went well. There were no mammoth sittings, the judges took an intelligent interest in the case and all the plane spotters who managed to make the journey were acquitted.

Except one... The oldest of the plane spotters suffered some sort of breakdown. Although he sent a medical certificate to the appeal court, together with a request that his appeal be heard in his absence, his plea was ignored and to this day he remains convicted. The situation is a disgrace and a presidential pardon to him should be granted immediately.

I caught up with Paul and Lesley Coppin at their home near Ely in November 2012. It was the first time I'd really seen the inside of their bungalow. The only other time I'd been there, ten years ago, it was high summer in the interval between the first trial and the appeal. The entire group had met up for a barbecue/council of war in the garden. Leslie looked much the same, but Paul was much fatter than I remembered him from when we first met shortly after prison. He told me he'd lost a stone-and-a-half because the food was so inedible.

We discussed their experiences of imprisonment. They were together in a police cell in Kalamata for two weeks before being transferred to different prisons – Paul to Nauplia, in the north of the Peloponnese, and Lesley to the only woman's prison in Greece, near Athens.

Paul told me that the police cell time did not trouble him. His morale was high because of the constant visits by dignitaries from Athens, including the Foreign Secretary, reflecting the tension between Athens and the locals. Besides, after the arrest, as I had found, the police switchboard had been totally jammed, so the prisoners got their own telephone line. Paul was giving interviews in the very beginning to the *Today* programme on the BBC and CNN, and all prisoners kept in touch with relatives and friends.

His morale plummeted on the move to prison. This was his bleakest period. Everybody, including the British ambassador, had assured them they would be out of there very quickly and it wasn't happening. He was worried about Lesley. He didn't hear from her for quite a while.

For the first week the group were just chucked into cells where there was space. 'I was in an overcrowded cell with nobody who could speak English,' he told me. 'They were all Greek.' From the second week onwards they were all together. He had no complaints about his treatment in prison, apart from the inedible food. Word had got out to both officials and other prisoners that they were to be properly treated and if anything happened to them, there would be serious trouble. 'We were untouchable.'

He went on: 'I was worried from time to time but I wasn't constantly depressed or anything like that. I realise compared to others we were treated very well. I was having a nasty, but not a terribly dreadful experience – it was the loss of liberty, and often being out of touch with Lesley.'

Lesley told me that she got rather shocked and distressed after the first court hearing on the Friday. The charges had been raised from misdemeanours with a maximum sentence of three years to twenty to twenty-five years for espionage.

On the Monday she received the first visit by the British Consul. By this time she was truly fighting mad. She said she told the diplomat, 'We have to provide our own bog paper and nobody has thought to send in any of the bloody stuff. You wait to hear about yourselves in the media tomorrow.' It was amazing how quickly things improved after that.

They'd been promised they could stay together in the police station whilst things were being sorted out. Suddenly police in riot squad gear made a dawn raid to avoid the attention of the media, and carted everybody off to prison.

'The whole thing was pretty awful. When I was being driven away I was in a car not a prison van. My imagination was overtaking my logic because things were going wrong at such a rapid rate.'

She was taken to Athens police station where they put her in a police cell that stank and was covered in pornographic graffiti.

'There were concrete beds. I wasn't alone and I began to get quite frightened.'

She thought she was in prison until one of the fellow inmates who spoke English told her prison would be better because 'I'd find sheets on the bed'.

On arrival at Greece's only women's prison near Athens, she was strip-searched 'with men going up and down the stairs and I was in the stairwell... The experience was very demeaning. It was in front of sixteen-year-old girls and my figure is no longer what it might be.'

But she also met with kindness. 'My first night in prison, I looked at the high-up top bunk and a lady from the bottom bunk bed gave it up because she saw I could not climb up there.'

Once there, she didn't eat or get off her bed for days, although the food was pretty good as a result of prison riots earlier in the year.

'The rest of the cellmates were so good to me. Whilst I was refusing to take food, whenever I went out of the cell to the toilet or somewhere I came back to find a little food treat waiting for me on my bed.'

A couple of meetings showed the change in her status as the clamour about the case progressed. One of the early visitors was her MEP. She was taken to the prison governor's office to meet him. He was asked whether he would like some coffee, and when he asked about her, was told the prisoners weren't offered coffee. He refused to take any, waited until the Governor's back was turned, and poured them both some.

A few days later she was again summoned to the governor's office, this time to meet the Greek Foreign Secretary and his international law adviser who told her, 'In Greece you will get justice... eventually.' The subject of coffee was again broached. 'This time the Governor was sent out to get the coffee for the rest of us!'

But then Greece is Greece and we do things so much better here. No Greek need ever worry about facing ridiculous terrorist charges in this country, right?

England: Charalambos Dousemetzis

Less than three months after the plane spotters returned home, Special Branch officers stormed into the Newcastle lodgings of Charalambos Dousemetzis, removing almost all of his belongings for further examination. He soon found himself in Durham high security prison accused of being a member of the November 17th movement, a Greek terrorist organisation that had recently murdered a British brigadier in Athens. A subservient Northumberland bench remanded him in custody for a month.

I heard of this peculiar case through the local media, who had found that the young Greek had been studying at Newcastle University for the previous eight years: the 'terrorist' material was in fact his notes for a projected doctorate, an investigation of the November 17th movement. A telephone call to his tutor should have resolved the issue but it was never made. I telephoned the Greek Embassy to obtain further information. They were very interested to hear what news I could give them since no one had ever contacted them to tell them they had a national arrested and imprisoned. As a result, the Ambassador called on an embarrassed Jack Straw to make an official protest about a clear breach of Consular law. On April 8th, 2003, a shamefaced Crown Prosecution Service withdrew all charges before the magistrates and the student flew home just in time for the Greek Easter, vowing to seek his doctorate elsewhere. What particularly aggrieved him was that he never got back the photograph from his wall. No doubt some bright spark in Special Branch circulated this image of a dangerous criminal to Interpol, complete with iconic baggy trousers and bowler hat. Interpol can withdraw the arrest warrant for Charlie Chaplin. He is buried in Switzerland.

11

Lorry Loads

By October 1994 it was clear that there was a pattern of injustice affecting the international trucking industry, centred on the inability of a trucker to examine the contents of his load. It was to became my major preoccupation over the next two or three years and continued to be of great concern throughout my watch.

The containerisation revolution had changed the nature of trucking. What was essential was the rig, the cab to which any form of trailer could be coupled. With the growth of international trade the trailers were over ten metres in length: the size and volume of a three-room flat. The trucker would arrive for his return load to find pre-packed trailers full of vast containers which he had no opportunity to examine.

There were two types of trucker. Employed truckers worked directly for major transport companies and were members of the Transport & General Workers Union (TGWU), the biggest trade union in Britain. There was also a trucking cottage industry, catered for by the United Road Transport Union (URTU). Many truckers bought a cab, usually on hire purchase, and worked from home with their wives doing the bookkeeping. Those who did international work established relationships through transport agents near their homes and were hired through them to take goods to France, Spain and beyond. It was a highly competitive business and the real profit was to be made in the agents finding a return load they could take back to Britain. Only rarely could a return load be arranged in advance. The trucker would deliver the outward load and contact the agent to see if and where a return load was available.

By the spring of 1995, David Higginbottom, secretary of URTU, Douglas Curtis, his press officer, Cornish and myself had worked out the parameters of the truckers' plight.

One morning I received a surprise telephone call from John Waite, brother of famous hostage Terry Waite and reporter/presenter of BBC radio investigative programme *Face the Facts*. He told me he was in the final throes of putting together a programme on that plight and he'd only just found out about my interest in the topic – could he come round immediately and record what I knew, so he could incorporate it in the programme?

I still have the old-fashioned Sony cassette that contains my recording of what turned out to be the most influential radio reportage in the history of FTA. John Waite had put together a powerful half-hour sound picture of a chorus of desperate misery and callous official indifference.

The programme started with an examination of the plight of John Jones, arrested for drug smuggling in Morocco – a bad place to be. I was quoted as saying: 'Horrific tales of lorry drivers having been beaten are quite public now... There is no justice system worthy of the name and you are entirely dependent on what diplomats can do for you'. His trial lasted a matter of minutes and ended with a five-year prison sentence and a £30,000 fine with another four years in default.

These are his words: *'You can imagine how I felt. I was completely devastated. I was suicidal. I couldn't see my wife. I just could not believe I was in this position for something I haven't done... People would switch themselves with tin lids – I'm not just talking about tiny cuts... There's no medical attention in there. They don't stitch them up and there's no hospital. I saw two Moroccans with TB. There's a pipe coming out of their chests emptying into a jam jar with a piece of string that they share... English guy in there has his tooth out with an adjustable spanner.'*

Luckily his MP, Ann Widdecombe, journeyed to Morocco and rescued him.

Another case was that of John Barber, who hauled a load of fish from Devon to Spain with a return load of Spanish tangerines.

When he failed to return one day in 1993 his wife Mitzi began to worry that he'd been in an accident.

It transpired that John Barber had been stopped in Bayonne with packets of cannabis among the fruit, charged with smuggling and put in jail.

In his own words: *'He took me right down to the end of this corridor and put me in cell 39... I was in tears. Near breaking point. I just sat on the bed quietly and cried my eyes out. I'm not ashamed to say that anyone in that sort of state would.'*

Abruptly and unexpectedly he was released after three or four months but the Barbers had been forced into bankruptcy. Their MP investigated and found the cargo of tangerines in which the drugs had been found had been sold and the rented trailer had been given back to its British owners. The French had been satisfied to lock up the driver and look no further.

Again I was quoted: *'That is all too often what happens. It seems to me that the legal systems of a number of countries including perhaps our own... believe that the lorry driver is proved guilty unless... he is somehow proved innocent.'*

The programme went on to examine the way the transport system actually works. It quoted David Higginbottom, secretary of URTU: *'The difficulties many lorry drivers have is that they are effectively excluded from the loading process... What we have to be aware of is that the loading process starts a long way down the supply chain system and at any stage in the process drugs could be secreted into any part of that load. '*

The main problem was groupage – a mixed cargo that is assembled by agents abroad for shipment to the UK. The trailer may be loaded and sealed waiting: the driver simply hitches it up. A chorus of truckers were recorded, all complaining about their powerlessness.

John Waite went on to examine a notorious case. Roy Clarke had been a professional lorry driver for over a quarter of a century. On his way back from a routine trip to Gibraltar he received a fax directing him to a factory near Malaga where he was to pick up a consignment of large concrete pipes. After he'd picked them up, the

Guardia Civil (Spanish police) forced him over to a petrol station only a few hundred metres down the road. He thought it was a routine stop for paperwork. They weren't interested in that. There must have been a tip off. They smashed the pipes with iron bars uncovering £7m of cannabis cunningly set into the concrete. Roy Clarke remained in prison for two years and never got his truck back.

As I explained on the radio programme: *'Common sense tells you that drug dealers who can get away with their goods carried by innocent people cut down on the possibility of blackmail and the secret leaking out. They get the damn thing carried without having to pay for it.'*

Enter the FCO with a statement that there was nothing much worth discussing: *'Your approach suggests that there is a problem for British lorry drivers caught up with drugs overseas. The facts do not support this. There are relatively few British lorry drivers in the countries you mention.'*

The proper course for those unjustly treated, says the FCO statement, is to tell a lawyer: *'Any prisoner abroad concerned that his case is not being properly investigated should inform his lawyer who has access to all the evidence and is the proper channel for pursuing such concerns with the local authorities.'*

Conditions in French and Spanish prisons are so good that few prisoners take advantage of the arrangements that exist to serve out their time in a British cell. About Bayonne prison, the Foreign & Commonwealth Office has no concerns at all: *'Our Consul last visited the prison in December. The prisoners appear well fed. A typical menu is mackerel with white wine, turkey with four vegetables and peaches in syrup...'*

At Dover docks, the Government statements went down rather badly. Another chorus of indignant drivers ended the programme.

As a result, a number of influential politicians made contact with me. Lord Willie Goodhart told me that his wife had heard the programme and was so concerned that he took the matter up in the House of Lords. It was also part of more than one subsequent committee enquiry.

Throughout the 1990s there were usually well over a hundred British and Dutch truckers locked up in the two French border prisons: Bayonne, near Spain, and Longueville, for the Pas de Calais and Belgium. Perhaps as many as half of them were innocent of any wrongdoing, and helpless.

Steve Bryant: Morocco

Steve Bryant is a case in point. A middle-aged, divorced trucker from Essex, he ended up in a Moroccan prison. The only supporters who fought for him from the beginning were his elderly parents.

In February 1994, he was on his way from Basle to Barcelona when he received a fax telling him to pick up some cargo in Tetouan, Morocco. His statement read: *I was told to back my trailer into a small exit, which blocked my view. Loading would take place that afternoon... I spent a couple of hours repairing the shattered exhaust on my cab in front and when I looked at the back found loading almost complete. I was then told to start my fridge.* But he still couldn't leave: he was to wait for the vet (his cargo was frozen squid), who never showed.

The following day. The first I knew I had a problem was when customs climbed into the back and showed me cannabis concealed in sealed cartons...

It was Steve's third trip to Morocco and he had told relatives and friends all about the customs harassment he suffered on the first two. He would have had to be mad to have gone there to smuggle after these experiences.

Steve was sentenced to eight years on his first trial, which was increased to ten years, the maximum, on appeal.

In 1995, after Steve's appeal had been rejected, his parents contacted me. It was my first Moroccan case. They wanted me to go to Morocco and combine a fact-finding mission with a visit to Steve. His father was too old to travel and his mother was dying of cancer. When I told them we did not have the funds to cover such a trip, they insisted on cashing their last insurance policy for £500 for me to use. It was not going to be enough, but Sally and I decided to make it a working holiday. We used our own money as a supplement.

We spent a week in two centres: Tangiers, near Steve's prison, and Rabat, the capital, where I hoped to meet the British Consul General and the Minister of Justice.

Tangiers in January was no holiday resort. On our first evening we sat in the dining room of a four-star beachside hotel. We stared transfixed as a tide of wind-driven rainwater poured under the closed French windows to soak the fitted carpets and lap around our ankles. We were never far from umbrellas for the entire visit.

We called on the Tangiers Consulate. The Union Jack fluttered over the main road from the balcony of a converted flat in a residential block. The two female British staff briefed us on lawyers and the situation of the European foreigners in the local prison. There was great cooperation between the local EU Consulates: they were looking after the Dutch as well as the British at the time. They spent their own time and money providing cooked chicken dinners to their charges on a weekly basis.

I visited Maitre Suard Lazarac, the lawyer of choice for British prisoners in Tangiers. She practised from a couple of rooms over a small shopping arcade in a relatively poor district. I was the only man in the waiting room, which was full of young and middle-aged women with shopping baskets. She specialised in family law, one of only two females practising at the Tangiers bar. It was extremely tough being a radical woman lawyer in this male-dominated profession but she did have one thing going for her. Her father was the senior judicial authority in the area, holding the office of Inspector of Judges. She got us a permit to visit Steve Bryant with the cooperation of the public prosecutor.

We waited in the prison yard surrounded by high concrete walls topped with barbed wire. Since they had male and female queues, I was separated from Sally. A prison truck arrived through the main gate. Chains of manacled prisoners tumbled out of the back, possessions bursting out of their plastic bags. The prisoners were not allowed to recover them. They were forced into line and led away. A roar of raised voices could be heard coming from the visitors' block. Sally was frightened by it; she thought it was a riot.

They let us into the visitors block in batches of thirty or so. Two sets of parallel bars from floor to ceiling divided the long barrack room. A guard patrolled the walkway between them. Everyone stood – there were no chairs for visitors. The roar had been the excited babble of relatives and prisoners shouting across the divide to make themselves heard.

The Chief Warder placed us at the end of the bars behind a curtained-off section. It gave us some physical privacy from the hubbub, but a government minder stood on our side of the curtain in the walkway.

We found Steve waiting for us. With his long grey hair and flowing beard he looked like an Old Testament prophet. As we shouted our exchanges of news, from home and about his prison conditions, he exuded dignity and charisma. He talked about the treatment of the other British prisoners, little about himself. Here was a prince in captivity, a natural leader of men. We had heard from the Consul how he was a father figure to the other inmates and a friend of the governor, who believed him to be innocent. Sally and I left personally involved in the struggle to free him and from then on Sally was emotionally engaged in the mission.

When Sally went shopping in the hotel gift shop, the proprietor, wearing the traditional Jewish skull-cap, noticed our name on the credit card and asked whether we were Jewish. He was curious as to why a British couple were staying in the hotel in January. When she explained my business, he suggested that if I cared to go alone to a nearby cafe the following day I might be able to get some inside knowledge of the way cannabis smuggling was arranged. A most curious suggestion, but it was clear that Sally had made contact with a leader of the powerful Jewish community in Morocco. When I turned up I was greeted by a couple of elderly Orthodox Jews. They explained to me that local business communities in corrupt partnership with the local customs officials controlled smuggling of all types of goods, including drugs.

Drugs could leave Morocco safely in two ways: suitcases full of cannabis carried across the porous borders of the Spanish enclaves on the Moroccan mainland on a daily basis, and Moroccan boats dropping cannabis in weighted waterproof bundles near the Spanish coast and telephoning the GPS location to the Spaniards. I may have noticed the absence of locals in prison on drug offences. The scores of British, Dutch and German truckers doing time in Morocco's jails constituted the largest number of EU prisoners: sacrificial scapegoats to satisfy the Ministry of Justice back in Rabat that Customs was doing its job.

The Rabat visit could have been useless. The Vice Consul in charge of relations with the Moroccan authorities was married to a Moroccan and had the same attitude as Leonie Vejijiva had towards native justice in Thailand. She believed that Moroccan justice was fair and could do no wrong. However, my EU connections were more useful. Through the Italian Embassy I had a hurried interview with the Permanent Secretary of the Ministry of Justice just before Friday prayers. He expressed concern about the plight of Steve Bryant and the European truckers generally and promised to look into it.

Back in the UK I had an early meeting with Steve Norris, the Bryants' Member of Parliament and a former Transport Minister. I managed to convince him that Steve deserved support and he began to do battle with the FCO on the Bryants' behalf.

At some stage I acquired a packet of inter-Consular departmental memoranda on the case. In April, an internal memorandum had been circulated regarding it and truckers generally. It started from the premise that if a poorly educated truck driver did not fill his pardon application with specific reference to violations of basic human rights, the FCO could ignore it. It added that in any event the position in Moroccan law must not be challenged because other innocent lorry drivers in other parts of presumably non-EU countries might also demand support. At the time there were cases of concern in Turkey and Bulgaria.

Another memorandum dated three days later directed the Moroccan Embassy to ignore the European approach that I had initiated on the truckers' behalf. At the same time a smarmy letter was sent by the Minister expressing his regrets to Steve Norris that he was unable to support the Bryants.

When Labour won the General Election of June 1997 and Robin Cook became Foreign Secretary, he immediately announced that Human Rights would be a guiding principle for the Foreign Office. The Consular Service had serious problems in coming to terms with the new FCO mission. The last letter from the FCO to me on Steve's case in 1997 made all the right noises. It concluded: *Consular Division regards the protection of the human rights of our nationals to be an important part of our role in defending the rights of Britons in trouble overseas. If, for any reason, we are worried that the local law may be in breach of International Law and that this may act against the interests or human rights of British nationals, Consular Division will take action.*

We persisted with this case doing everything we could think of. Steve's mother died shortly after I returned from Morocco. He was still in prison when his father followed her to the grave. Meanwhile, Steve led his fellow Europeans on hunger strike against the prison conditions in Tangier and all foreigners were transferred to the Sale prison near the capital, Rabat, where the European Consul General could keep an eye on them. We made him 'Prisoner of the Month' for the third time in 2003. Morocco eventually released him just before Christmas of that year under a general amnesty. He'd served nine of the ten years of his sentence.

Spain: Steven Toplass

By 2005, almost at the end of my watch, we were a team of three full-time professionals supported by a few volunteers and part time ancillary staff. The basic casework was being done by Sabine Zanker, our German head of legal services. Here she uncovered a very British disgrace, an Orwellian nightmare. This case still beggars belief.

On the surface, the story of Steven John Toplass appears to be

that of the classic, duped truck driver abroad. A trucker of some
twenty years experience, Steven was hired early in 2004 by Cameron
Moir, a British citizen, for a one-off job. He was to take Cameron's
cab and closed trailer to Algeciras in Spain, pick up a load and return
with it to the UK. He duly turned up at the depot in Spain. As soon
as the loading began, he was ordered away from the loading bay and
made to wait six hours until it was finished and the trailer sealed.
Just as he set off to drive the goods home, he was arrested by local
Spanish police, who found 400 kilos of hash hidden at the back of
the trailer.

Of course, there was no way that Steven could have known that
Moir was the mastermind of a drugs gang and that the authorities
were on to him. By this time all his phone conversations were being
monitored by the British National Crime Squad. As a result, in the
hands of our police were:

- Telephone calls showing Steven's concern about not being
  present at the loading, the delay and Moir's reassurances to
  him
- A transcript of a telephone conversation between Moir and
  an accomplice saying 'the driver (Steven) is not friendly to
  our situation'.

The intention of the British police had always been to let Steven
return the load to Britain, so that they could catch Moir red-handed.
In the event, Moir and the other six members of his gang were
rounded up eleven days after Steven's arrest in Spain.

British police officers travelled twice to Alicante (where he was
imprisoned), once in late February 2004 and again in June 2004. On
both occasions they made stringent efforts to inform the Spanish
investigating authorities – and the investigating magistrate in particular
– about their intelligence, which confirmed Steven Toplass had been
used to transport the drugs without his knowledge. They showed their
Spanish counterparts detailed documentation, arising from the
intensive investigation. Our police were told that these matters had to

be taken up by the defence. This was rubbish. In Spain, as in France, it is the duty of police and public prosecutors to place before the magistrates all the evidence available. Some sort of attempt to contact the defence lawyer failed, and there they left it. They did not even bother to tell the British Consular service of Steven's plight. It was left to us to do this when we were eventually contacted.

Barely a month after the second police visit, Steven was convicted. He was sentenced to three-and-a-half years in prison and fined 600,000 Euros (£500,000), with a further six months inside if he couldn't pay.

It wasn't until the beginning of May 2005 that he saw an English translation of the judgement for the first time. At the trial, only the questions to him were translated into English, and vice versa. Since Steven had no idea what else was said in court, he had no opportunity to correct any mistakes or join in his own defence. The whole trial lasted no longer than one and a half hours.

An appeal was lodged and dismissed in November 2004. Both judgements noted that it was impossible to identify who was behind the company Accor Europe Ltd., who owned the truck. Yet a simple Google search under the name would have led the Spanish investigating team directly to Moir and his full contact details. In addition, the Spanish authorities were in touch with the leasing company, who claimed ownership of the lorry and they also had all the details they needed to track down the owner. The Spanish authorities never made contact with their British counterparts with a request for any information.

The defence lawyer, Mr Agustin Ribera, presented the judge in Alicante with a letter from Crown Prosecutor, Andrew Penhale, to Stephen Toplass dated 24th November, 2004, in which he informs him about their investigation of Moir and where he explicitly confirms that there is no evidence for prosecuting him as a part of the conspiracy. On the other hand, he voices the intention of the CPS to use his evidence as part of the prosecution case against others involved in the criminal trial in the UK. This letter was also translated into Spanish. First the judge would not recognise the logo of the CPS on the letterhead as genuine. When the letter was authenticated by the FCO, the judge still refused any action. It was clear that the Spaniards had their man and couldn't be bothered any more.

It was not until 25th November, the day after the CPS letter to Steve, that the British police finally got permission to see Steven in prison and a meeting took place with Spanish and British police in attendance. Only then, after the appeal was over, was Steven informed that the National Crime Squad were aware that he had been used as a 'mule' and that they had been tracking Moir for some time but wanted to catch him with the drugs.

The following March (2005) an agreement was made between the Spanish and British authorities to allow the temporary return of Steven to the UK. This would be for a total of up to two months from the beginning of April to give evidence in the trial against the Moir gang. Steven was sent to England on April 6th and was imprisoned in HMP Hull until May 24th, when he was returned to Spain in fulfilment of the bilateral agreement. In the end Moir and his gang all offered guilty pleas at trial: four of them, Moir included, only after the start of the proceedings at Leeds Crown Court. It was Steven's willingness to give evidence that made them change their minds. This was confirmed to FTA in a letter by Andrew Penhale, the same man who had written to the Spanish trial judge.

Moir was sentenced to three-and-a-half years imprisonment, of which he had to serve half, so in practice he was to serve less time in prison than Steven.

It was not until the spring of 2005 that Steve's partner, Diane, contacted us from Stoke-on-Trent. Although Sabine got to work immediately, it still took some time for her to get the evidence required to prove the tortuous string of events. By now we were in the throes of the June 2005 General Election. According to Diane, the previous local MP had been of little help but June 2005 saw Robert Flello elected for the seat. I admired him for the energy he put into this case whilst still trying to find his feet in the House of Commons. I launched the public side of the campaign nationally with an article in *The Times*. All this was news to the FCO, who immediately agreed that something had gone seriously wrong. I began to push the FCO to arrange a pardon. The FCO had strangled itself with a self-induced protocol that required them to get external legal advice from their panel on the case. It delayed official support for some months. Things only moved when a new British Consul General to Madrid met with me before taking up his appointment and promised to do his best. Steven eventually got his pardon nine days before he was due for release anyway. I never heard from him afterwards and I don't blame him. From his point of view a fat lot of use we were.

The virtues and importance of international cooperation in the investigation of crime had been a prime focus of the European Council for a decade. In particular Eurojust, the European equivalent of Interpol, was established specifically for dealing with cross border criminal problems such as this one. There was nothing unusual about the type of police operation. It is known as a controlled delivery. The authorities get intelligence that a drug consignment is being moved from country to country and it acts as a sort of flypaper. When the consignment arrives at its destination everyone who has had contact with it on its journey is rounded up.

What happened here was that despite the cross border nature of the operation, the local British police had not informed either Europol or their Spanish counterparts in advance. Even the Home Office, nominally the government department responsible, did not have a system of control and were not aware of Steven's plight. When the operation was aborted by Steven's arrest in Spain, the Home Office and Foreign Office should have been informed immediately. It was all a cover up at Steven's expense.

And no one lived happily ever after. In December 2012, I travelled to Stoke-on-Trent to interview Steven's wife, Diane Toplass. She met me at the station looking extremely smart in red, and drove us the couple of miles to her local pub. We chatted together about our families and backgrounds: we both have two children and three grandchildren. Over lunch, she began to tell me their story...

They had only been together for about five months when he got arrested. It wasn't the first relationship for either of them. She had married very young and had two adult children by this time, and it was Steven's third marriage.

Her nightmare all started with a phone call that she received on Saturday, 7th February, 2004. 'The person on the other end of the line spoke broken English. At first I thought it was a bit of a wind-up until Steven came on the line and said: "I've only got thirty seconds. I've been arrested". For about half an hour, I just stared into space. I kind of broke down, really. I was that shocked I didn't know what to do.'

Diane tracked down Moir immediately. 'I went to see him. I was very distraught and at the time didn't realise that Moir's comments were a bit strange.'

She contacted the British Consulate on the Saturday to be told that nothing could be done over the weekend. Steven was to appear before a court within three days in Alicante.

'I wasn't sure where Alicante was and had no way of getting in contact with Steve until the following Wednesday.'

She contacted Moir again and he said he would get hold of a Spanish lawyer.

'I just didn't know what to do. I was lost.'

After about a week she was beginning to get suspicious of Moir. Then she was informed that he had been arrested.

'He'd been kidding me along that he was going to see about a lawyer. Steve was represented at court by some sort of court liaison.'

Diane managed a visit to the prison at the end of the month.

'It was a round-trip over the weekend. It cost me a few hundred pounds because I could only travel during school breaks and it was the high-season price. It was just us and quite a frightening experience.'

The Foreign Office had fixed her up with papers for the Spa-niards, telling them she was Steven's partner.

'The first time I saw him in prison it was only three or four weeks since I'd last seen him, but I was really shocked. He'd lost perhaps two stone in such a short time and he was quite unrecognisable. In

Spain you get "conjugal time" in prison, but our time was quite fraught. Steve was very anxious, asking me to get things, while I was trying to tell him what I'd done. He couldn't even get phone cards.'

He needed a lawyer. Before Steven's arrest Diane had her own house free of mortgage: it was her security. She started with a small mortgage to pay the legal fees, but then there were the costs of visiting.

'I saw him three or four times a year. I still flew at high season rates. It was costing me so much money that I had to take a week in Benidorm as a package holiday, since that was the nearest place to Steve's prison.'

Transport then became a major problem. In the end, the various costs of looking after Steve drove her into bankruptcy and she lost the house.

'In the beginning I thought I was going to wake up and all would be well. I put a lot of faith in the people I was contacting and thought that officials would soon realise it was all a mistake and Steve would be sent home. It took me two or three months for things to sink in.'

We picked up the story again:

'I wasn't at the meeting in Spain when it was arranged for him to come back to England to give evidence. There were some half promises, though: when he did get back they'd find a way of releasing him. He certainly firmly believed that they were going to get him out. I was pretty sure at the time they could sort the mess out. He'd been over there a year...

'He was here [in the UK, for Moir's trial] for six to eight weeks. I saw him every week at the prison. When the trial was over they wrapped him up very quickly and sent him back because they promised Spain they would do that. I know that the governor of the prison at the time wanted to keep Steve and supported him, but was overruled by the CPS because of the agreement.'

I said that what surprised many people involved was that neither she nor Steven had got in touch with them after it was all over. Diane said that Steven had not gone back to anyone.

'He had to pick himself up and go to work.'

Diane and I discussed FTA involvement. She knew we were working hard – she'd been to a couple of the meetings with officials in London – but she didn't realise that we had roused Europe. We convened a special meeting with the Justice Commissioner to discuss the total lack of liaison between the British and Spanish authorities. I told her that from our end it was when Sabine got through to the Special Branch sergeant who blew the whistle on the prosecutions' lacklustre performance that changed everything. It had taken us about three months to realise the awful truth.

This was the only case we had ever come across where the British Government had played such an active role in assisting a miscarriage of justice. I told her what really worried me about life after Steven's return was that she had pursued a claim for compensation for three years and it had gone nowhere. She replied that in the end she got so fed up, she just gave up. She didn't have the papers and Steven eventually took them. She didn't even know whether they had ever had an offer or not or whether they'd issued a writ.

Things did not work out for them after Steven came out. It became an on-off relationship and they first split up within three or four months.

'Things were too difficult. I suppose I was expecting some Mills & Boon [ending], I was expecting the romance because of the letters we exchanged.'

They got together again quite quickly after the first split. Then they married in April, 2008, and moved house.

'. . . and then we split again – we aren't really in touch. It's hard to think about. I no longer think about it every day, it's hard to survive. People need to know what this sort of thing does to victims' lives. It costs heavy.'

I left full of admiration for this highly intelligent, brave woman.

By international convention, the captain and crews of commercial carriers of goods by air and sea were exempt from prosecution and responsibility for illicit cargoes unless evidence of personal involvement existed. These conventions did not apply to yacht delivery crews.

Spain: Paul Humble and Gregory Saxby

Paul lived aboard a large charter motor vessel in Almira, Spain, which he maintained for the English owner. In January 1998, Paul was given the job of taking the boat to Malta via Gibraltar and invited his friend Gregory to join him. At Gibraltar, the agent for the owner informed them that the plans were changed. A fresh crew was to take their boat over off the coast of Morocco and they were to return by another boat that would pick them up. While waiting for the new crew, they were boarded by police and accused of being concerned with smuggling a large quantity of cannabis into Morocco. No evidence of the cannabis was ever produced. Both men were sentenced to ten years on the say-so of the police.

12

Uncle Joe's Legacy

In 1994, I was involved in the first of our Eastern European cases. Democracy may have come to the old Soviet Block, but the legal systems hadn't changed.

East Germany: David Kidd

The recession of the early 1990s forced the British construction worker to look elsewhere for employment. Popular television culture had already comically chronicled the stampede of the unemployed building tradesmen in *Auf Wiedersehen, Pet*, showing men fleeing from unemployment in Liverpool and Newcastle to the new El Dorado of Germany during the 1980s.

One of the regular 'guest workers' was thirty-seven-year-old David Kidd, of Reading. In 1994, David and a group of his British mates decided to have a night out at a Stendal disco. Since he was the driver, David wasn't drinking, but a tipsy friend got into some sort of quarrel with the local youngsters and things were turning ugly. David managed to haul his friend outside and bundled him into the passenger seat of his car, hotly pursued by a bunch of local youths. In his panic, he drove off on the British side of the road and clipped a female cyclist coming the other way. She suffered a broken leg.

It was perhaps fortunate for him that the police arrived and protected him. What he couldn't understand was that he was charged with attempted murder and was told by his lawyer that he was facing a possible sentence of twenty years for what he believed was a traffic accident. I think it was David Rendel, Mr Kidd's local MP, who contacted me first. We were soon joined by his MEP, John Stevens. The German lawyer applied for bail and it turned out that the vociferous witnesses were all members of a neo-Nazi youth group, who hated the foreign immigrant workers for taking jobs that belonged to good Germans. Most of them had criminal records involving physical violence. It was a very bad choice of bar for the Brits to relax in!

In an astonishing turn of events, the local judge refused the bail application on the grounds that he was far too busy trying murder cases. This was only an attempted murder case and anyway, bail applications would have to wait their turn. The lawyer reported back to us that it was likely to be several weeks before he would get the chance to make the application. I simply could not understand how a German judge, in a Premier League country for fair trial, could take such a cavalier attitude to the priorities of a bail application. John Stevens discussed the matter with his German colleagues in the European Parliamentary Conservative group. He discovered that, although the reunification of Germany had taken place nearly four years before, the local criminal justice system administrators and judges had remained untouched in the area that used to be the German Democratic Republic – and Stendal used to be in East Germany.

After a major article in the *Daily Mail*, Kidd's lawyer found himself making a bail application before a very different court. The judicial authorities had stuffed the court with West German judges, who behaved as one would expect. Bail was granted and conditions progressively eased with each hearing until Kidd was flying from home to attend the hearings. When the court-appointed expert reported that at the time of the collision the car was moving slower than the cyclist, the criminal case collapsed and the charge was reduced to careless driving. Kidd pleaded guilty and was fined a couple of hundred pounds. The presiding judge then informed Kidd he had assessed the damages for false imprisonment for a much larger sum and awarded him the difference.

This was the case that taught me the real value of the European Parliament in pursuing justice for clients within the European Union. It wasn't the direct power that mattered; they had none. It was the ability, in this case, of a British MEP to confer with his German colleagues and persuade them to approach their own authorities. From then on I acted as link between clients and their MEPs and advised the MEPs concerned on the breaches of law in their cases. The collegiate nature of Parliament helped us to obtain results in cases across Europe from Greece to Spain over the coming years.

It was also the beginning of another lesson. Persisting differences in culture and mentality among the old East Germany and old West Germany are often referred to as the 'wall in the head' (*mauer im kopf*). Twenty years after the fall of the wall, only twenty-two per cent of former East Germans considered themselves 'real citizens of the Federal Republic'. Sixty-two per cent felt in a kind of limbo, no longer citizens of East Germany but not fully integrated into the unified Germany.

Russia: Karen Henderson

Karen Henderson, like Karyn Smith before her, was just eighteen when she arrived at a Moscow airport from Cuba in the early hours of February 6th, 1996. Police said 3,900 grams of cocaine were found in a false compartment of her new suitcase. Half-Dutch, she was travelling with a fellow Dutch woman, aged twenty-four, who pleaded guilty to drug smuggling.

Karen's story in court, backed up by evidence, was that she had set off during the holidays from her home in Holland to travel around the Caribbean. She was looking for a place to study as part of a programme at her college. From there, she intended to travel to Poland to visit the mountain ski resort of Zielona Góra, but it was cheaper for her to fly with Aeroflot via Moscow. Her story was that just before she left Cuba her suitcase broke, so she had to buy another one with the help of an airport official whom she had never met before. She was not given the luggage ticket when she registered her luggage, but a tag was attached to her suitcase which certified to whom it belonged. Somewhere between baggage registration and her passing through passport control she was invited to have her luggage examined. During the search at Havana airport, nothing unusual was discovered in the suitcase. She did not see her luggage again until she arrived in Moscow more than twenty-four hours later. The subsequent discovery of drugs in her suitcase came as a great shock. Certainly, having been found with a large amount of cocaine in a secret compartment, Karen had a case to answer, but her story needed dealing with in court by an adequate prosecution.

The trial system in Moscow was a variant of the German criminal system, a judge sitting with two assessors. The Soviets dealt with the independent assessor problem by appointing good party people on their retirement. The OAPs in Karen's case tended to fall asleep during the trial sessions, the interpretation provided was wholly inadequate, and despite Karen's personal protestations, the incomprehensible trial continued. None of the exhibits, such as the suitcase or drug packets, were produced in court. The arresting customs official did not turn up and the reports produced about the contents of the alleged drug packets showed that more than ten per cent of the cocaine had disappeared between the dates of two reports.

At the conclusion of the defence evidence, the court rejected Karen's case on the grounds that it contradicted ordinary logic, coupled with a hypothetical conclusion. '*The only possible explanation for Karen Henderson's decision to fly from Havana to Poland via Moscow, despite the possibility of shortening it by changing flights in Dublin, is that her arrival on the flight from Moscow was expected.*' No one had bothered to examine the defence evidence or counter it with evidence for the prosecution, since there had been none. What occurred at her trial in the autumn of 1996 was a reflection of a totally unreformed hangover from the Soviet era where convictions occurred on the prosecutor's say-so. The Russians have always reproached themselves on their periodic public 'skandals' and here was a judicial example. On 17th October, 1996, Karen was sentenced to six years hard labour.

In March 1997, I received a letter from Karen's mother, a Dutch citizen, asking for help. She told me an appeal against the conviction was due to be heard in April, although it was eventually determined in September when a retrial before a different tribunal was ordered. The Henderson parents asked me to go on a forty-eight-hour fact-finding mission to Moscow to check on lawyers and the Russian legal system.

The flight to Moscow took about five hours. It took me another five hours queuing to get into Moscow past the solitary immigration officer coping with several planeloads of passengers. Welcome to Yeltsin's dysfunctional Russia.

I arrived at the Beograd (Belgrade), a three-star hotel in the centre of Moscow at 11pm. My body clock told me it was suppertime and I was directed to the only hotel restaurant still open, a Greek taverna, and given a small table next to a roaring log fire. By then it was midnight. The teenage waitresses were all dressed in Greek costumes but the skirts were thigh-length. The tiny dance floor was packed with couples smooching to piped Greek music. Although I was in my early sixties, I was about the youngest male in the place. What a charming scene: every table had a grandfather taking his granddaughter out to dinner... The food was good but the waitresses, who spoke no English, seemed to think I was short of company. I was lonely, as I usually was on these investigative trips, but not that lonely!

The next morning I went with Karen's mother to the British Embassy to meet the Consul General and his staff. The diplomat responsible for prison visiting was extremely concerned about the conditions Karen was being held under. Whilst she hadn't been moved to a labour camp, where conditions were even worse, the prison was a nightmare. Karen was herded into a cell with fifty others and kept there twenty-three hours out of twenty-four. TB and hepatitis were rife. During the year and a half she had been in prison, the authorities refused to allow any communication that was not in the Russian language, so unless there was a personal visit she was cut off from communication with the outside world. Every time she went to court she was woken at 4am, collected from the prison cell at 5am and eventually arrived at court about noon. She did not return to her cell until midnight and was not allowed any food or rest during this time. If the hearing lasted more than one day, the process was repeated each day, and as a consequence she was tired, starving and not in a fit state to communicate with the lawyers.

That evening I met Karen's lawyers, Alla Zhivina, the vice-chairman of the Moscow bar, and Karina Moskalenko, director of the Human Rights Institute. It was a pleasure to meet two lawyers who would have prospered as defence lawyers in any advanced legal system. Karen's treatment in prison had been of such concern to them that they raised complaints to the United Nations Commission on Human Rights on her behalf. To their minds, there was torture in that she had received selective ill-treatment and if she pleaded guilty she would get better conditions in prison. There were constant body searches, including intimate body parts, every time she went to and from court and indeed on other occasions.

They explained to me the conditions under which they worked and the eclectic nature of the numerous separate criminal justice systems that operated within the Russian Federation. There was no uniform legal system even between districts within the country of Russia itself. Moscow District employed non-jury trial systems for criminal offences, whilst in Rostov jury trials prevailed.

A simple visit to confer with the client in prison was a logistical nightmare. Permission to interview was easily obtained, but the lack of interview rooms for lawyers to meet in was appalling. Although the Moscow central remand prison had many thousands of prisoners awaiting trial and all needing to see their lawyers, there were only three single lawyers' conference rooms, let out on a first-come, first-served basis. No reservation was possible. Lawyers had to queue for several hours in order to see their clients. They had to 'hire' the visiting room by paying over £100 for the visit. The bulk of this went to the State and the prison authorities. Only the so-called 'businessmen' could afford the luxury of seeing their lawyers before trial.

At any stage, the examining magistrate could send the case file back to the investigative branch for further examination even during the trial. This created lengthy delays and happened several times in Karen's case. The entire system was in chaos. Files were lost. One of these women's clients, a Dutchman, had been convicted of a homicide charge without any evidence before the court since both the file and the homicide weapon had been lost. The higher courts were careful about defendants' rights under the Constitution and that's why, in Karen's case, a retrial was ordered.

At the time of my visit, the retrial was underway and had been adjourned to 14th October. A number of British reporters had been to the trial and reported some fairly obvious mistakes that had occurred on the first day. We all agreed it wasn't helpful to comment on the current trial whilst it was running. This might affect a relatively favourable outcome, but it might prove difficult to hold the line. It was possible the trial could be adjourned for further investigation and run for several months, so the agreed strategy was to go quietly until the conclusion of the trial and the announcement of the inevitable sentence. We hoped that the sentence on her would be something that in practice would enable her to be released.

The next day I attempted to pay my hotel bill on the ground floor. I was again unintelligibly pestered by ladies whilst waiting for attention, but was then directed to the desk on my room floor. Each floor of the hotel had been leased to a separate company.

In October, Tony Blair raised the case with Boris Yeltsin during a state visit. At the final hearing of the retrial, just before Christmas, Karen astonished the court with an impassioned outburst asserting her innocence. She was sentenced to one year eleven months – time served.

Romania: Graham Giles

In the late 1980s, a Baptist minister in Plymouth, Graham Giles became aware of the plight of Romanian children and moved to Romania to work with them. He was horrified at the prison conditions he found there. He also became director of Partnership For Justice, which he ran from the provincial town of Arad, and was adviser to the Romanian Minister of Justice, who was a civilian, on probation matters.

In December 1997, Graham was taking a child to hospital to have artificial legs fitted when he was involved in a road accident. The female passenger in the other car, who was not wearing a seatbelt, was fatally injured. The driver of the car had no driving licence or insurance. He was also drunk, speeding and on the wrong side of the road. The other driver only faced simple charges of driving without a licence and being over the limit. He was no stranger to driving under the influence, having a record of at least two previous convictions. Graham, on the other hand, was charged with manslaughter and grievous bodily harm. The technical evidence and the witnesses supported Graham. After a farcical trial, Graham was convicted of manslaughter and given a suspended sentence of eighteen months. Welcome to Romanian justice.

In September 1998, shortly after the trial had begun and been adjourned, the charity Europe to Europe, 'parent' of Partnership for Justice, invited me to come to Arad. I was to address a local probation services conference on right to fair trial and to consult with Graham's lawyer and other British and Romanian local sources. The lawyer said that the prosecution was a disgrace, but there was no chance of Graham being acquitted locally and one would have to wait for an appeal to be heard in Sofia before justice might be done.

When I arrived at an old imperial hunting lodge, now being used as a conference centre, I was put up for the night in the main bedroom. The bedroom was the size of a ballroom, the main feature being a king-size bed. The adjacent bathroom was the size of a normal bedroom. Occupying most of the wall above the huge bath was a water system with so many valves and levers it looked like the interior of the driver's cabin in an old-fashioned steam engine. I spent a quiet night. When I woke up in the morning, I was told that the bed had been used by the imperial prince who had been assassinated, the Ceausescus, and Marshal Tito. I no longer believe in ghosts.

The probation conference was running with military precision, but then it was a military occasion. All those in the probation service were military officers. The military were responsible for running the prisons, and the Romanian probation service was an extension of the prison system. We were all kept waiting – the military sitting to attention – for Colonel Bucur, commander of the local prison services, to arrive and make a keynote speech.

There was apparently a political battle going on between those who saw the new probation services as a civil authority within the Ministry of Justice, where one would expect it to be, and those who were trying to annex it to the Romanian prison service. There were, for example, requirements that the prison officers go on tank-driving courses, which appeared to sit somewhat uneasily with customary probation service training.

The Minister for Justice had just appointed a senior civil servant to be responsible for probation services. The Army appeared to have stolen a march on them with the appointment of Colonel Bucur to be responsible for the same services. Giles, clearly identified as a local supporter of the Ministry, was a covert target of the local military that had a vested interest in ensuring his conviction and tarnishing the civilian takeover.

Bulgaria: Peter Hobbs and John Mills

Names are forgettable: lawyers use pigeonholes to remember the names involved in their old cases. It was easy to retrieve this one, given the coincidence that both defendants had the same surnames, give or take an 'e', as famous British philosophers. All I had to do was remember it as the 'philosopher's case', the Leviathan, a heavy goods vehicle.

Peter Hobbs and John Mills, both from East London, were arrested on the Bulgarian side of the Turkish-Bulgarian border in 1995. The facts of the case troubled me. Twenty kilos of heroin were found in an unlocked compartment on the outside of their rig, to which anyone could have had access. They'd been searched and cleared on the Turkish side of the border. Two years earlier, in 1993, Nicky Chinn, a fifty-five-year-old driver from Scarborough, North Yorkshire, was arrested on the Turkish side of the border in disturbingly similar circumstances. He too carried a consignment of motor vehicle spare parts to Turkey from Britain and was ordered back via the same route with his empty lorry to pick up another load in Romania. Seven-and-a-half kilos of heroin was found in an unlocked outer compartment of his vehicle.

There was also another case, virtually identical, involving two Enfield lorry drivers on the Bulgarian side of the border. The same Turkish-controlled import-export company was concerned in all three.

Late in 1997, the BBC's legal correspondent Jon Silverman and I found a window of opportunity to make a mini documentary involving Brits accused of smuggling through Eastern Europe. By this time Hobbs and Mills had been processed through a farcical trial. In the middle of the trial it dawned on the judge that there might be a conflict of interest between the two, so he appointed a new lawyer to ensure separate representation, but the case was immediately continued without the new boy being given any opportunity to talk to his client and find out what the case was about. Both truckers were sentenced to seven-and-a-half years in jail.

The British police had sent a letter of support for Peter Hobbs to the Bulgarian authorities but it had been completely ignored at the trial, so we decided to approach the case through Peter. His brother Stanley and sister-in-law Shirley were grateful for the chance to visit Peter, since the only communication had been by monthly letters. I was extremely interested to get the opportunity to see the Bulgarian justice system first-hand and have the chance to meet the state prosecutor.

We had an appointment with the chief state prosecutor, his HQ a featureless, neo-brutalist building in the centre of the city. The BBC party, which included Stanley and Shirley, was running about five minutes late and our charming female interpreter and guide was visibly shaken and worried that we weren't on time. As we walked down an endless bare corridor, I noticed a high velocity bullet hole in one of the windows.

With the Hobbs party looking on, we started the interview with a Molotov clone exuding oppressive charm in Bulgarian. It was a bizarre display of omnipotence by someone who obviously didn't care what we in the West thought of Bulgarian justice. I started off with the concept of presumption of innocence, which he said he understood. I then pointed out that we had heard there were approximately a hundred cases a year involving smuggling, and no one had heard of anyone acquitted since the change of regime in 1990. He agreed with me that if that was right, the presumption of innocence wasn't working very well. There must have been innocent people in such a series, even though we couldn't tell which ones. He said my information was incorrect and sent an aide to investigate. Shortly before the end of the interview the aide returned shaking his head.

One of the bits of the interview left on the BBC cutting room floor was a passage in which I attempted to find out who determined the guilt or innocence of defendants. He said it was he and his department. I said surely that was the function of the trial judge and assessors. He said yes, in theory, but in practice the trial judge wouldn't acquit anyone he sent for trial on the grounds that it might belittle him, the state prosecutor, and the efficiency of his office.

There was another incident that told us where power and authority truly lay in the new democratic Bulgaria. The BBC was filming my arrival at the hotel for the umpteenth time when a police car drove up, sirens blaring. A couple of police ordered the film crew to stop filming and clear out from the front of the hotel – all this so that the Sofia chief of police could park his car in front of the building whilst he attended a function inside.

We did manage a visit to the prison, a grim, mid-nineteenth century relic. The Hobbs were expecting a prison visit across an ordinary table. They were faced with layers of glass and chicken wire on either side of a walkway as barriers between visitor and prisoner, so the only way to communicate was by telephone. We managed to arrange a visit, later in the morning, face-to-face in the Governor's office, as a special concession. The only way to describe Peter and John, with their gaunt, starved faces and multiple layers of warm clothing, was as convicts in a Siberian gulag; they had both visibly lost several stone. They were not complaining about brutality: it was the cold of a Bulgarian winter without a working heating system, meaning that icicles formed on the inside of their cells every night.

Perhaps as a result of the publicity surrounding the screening of the documentary in February 1998, their appeal was held later that year and a retrial was granted before the original court. In the retrial they were re-convicted, but other obvious breaches of the European Convention on Human Rights occurred. Their legal remedy was to re-appeal, but they were clearly in what chess players would call a 'perpetual check situation'. The Bulgarian justice system was at the stage where the superior courts were applying the ECHR, which had been incorporated into Bulgarian law after the fall of the Communist regime, but the inferior courts – as with the state prosecutor – were applying the old rules and Mills and Hobbs were being yo-yoed between the two. The only way to get them home was to abandon the court proceedings and apply for a Presidential pardon.

On 10 September 1999, having obtained that pardon and served four-and-a-half years of their sentence, Peter Hobbs and John Mills arrived in Heathrow's Terminal 2.

Bulgaria: Michael Shields

A decade after the arrest of the philosophers, I was observer at the trial of another Briton in Bulgaria, which demonstrated how slow the pace of reform was.

2005 was a great year for Liverpool fans. A loyal army of supporters travelled to Turkey to see their team win the European Champions' League. A number of tour companies arranged a stopover break on the way back in Varna, a Bulgarian holiday resort on the Black Sea. As one would expect, there was a great deal of raucous, inebriated behaviour late at night but surprisingly little in the way of major incidents. That is, until one fan committed a serious crime.

Early one morning, someone dropped a piece of paving slab on the head of Bulgarian waiter Martin Georgiev, as he tried to break up a brawl outside a takeaway kebab shop. Georgiev, father of a two-year-old son, lost a five-centimetre piece of his skull in the attack and suffered permanent brain damage. A number of Liverpool supporters were pulled in by the police, two of them – Graham Sankey and Michael Shields – staying at the same hotel. Graham Sankey was released and allowed to return home. On the plane back he was heard boasting of what he had got away with. Meanwhile, Michael Shields had been arrested, charged and sent for trial on a charge of attempted murder.

Long before the trial, I was contacted by the Shields family to assist and it was clear that the Bulgarians had got the wrong man. We made strenuous efforts to get them to issue an international arrest warrant for Sankey, who had a history of violence in the UK. The court refused to implement any enforcement action to get him before the court, even though he made a sensational confession on affidavit through a solicitor just as the trial was beginning. I spoke to Sankey's solicitor and there was no doubt in my mind we were talking about the same incident. No other incident of this nature had been reported to the police.

I was the only non-Bulgarian legal observer during the evidence stage of Michael Shields' trial. Almost all the formalities of fair trial were observed. So efficient was the simultaneous translation for both defendant and public that I was able to take verbatim notes of the proceedings, in exactly the same way that I would be able to in a British court. The defence lawyer was allowed to make applications and submissions just as the prosecutor was.

I have never attended a show trial as such before and it was not until the second day that I realised how it was being worked. All applications by the defence were refused. All applications by the prosecution, no matter how unreasonable, were granted. For example, a letter was produced by the prosecution signed by the Governor of the local prison and his secretary. It stated that shortly before the trial was due to begin Michael Shields had applied to the Governor to have his hair cut short. In their opinion, this was in order to avoid identification at trial. The defence requested that this document should not be admitted in evidence without the Governor and his secretary attending trial for the purposes of cross-examination. The defence application was refused and the letter was admitted as evidence.

Above all, the original eyewitness identification was 'improved'. Witnesses could contradict their first police statements. Then they could not remember details of the defendant's face. The defence were not allowed to put the police statements to the witnesses in cross-examination. Everyone was allowed to make dock identification as though this was of real evidential worth. It was clear, by her own evidence, that the only person who picked Shields out at an identification parade had had no opportunity of seeing his face at the time of the incident.

When I got home, the family and I were taken by their indefatigable MP Louise Ellman, for a meeting with Foreign Secretary Jack Straw. He was extremely sympathetic. However, it was clear there wasn't very much he could do.

I told the family that with Jack on our side we should be able to effect Michael's return to the UK, and from there find a way to have him set free. There was no help to be had from the Bulgarian authorities but the family had to go through the motions of the Bulgarian appeals system.

Two battles ensued: on one side the Liverpool community as a whole, on the other the Bulgarian and British governments. Councillor Joe Anderson, head of the Labour Party group on the Council, led for Liverpool, together with the city's MPs and MEPs. Cllr

Anderson was one of those heroic backers willing to sacrifice all in the interests of the cause. He was instrumental in raising the vast amount of money that had been fixed by the Bulgarian courts as the ransom for Michael's return. At one point he even told Jack Straw that he was prepared to resign from active politics in order to continue his efforts to get Michael released. He continued as a key factor in his rehabilitation after the pardon came through.

In October 2005, Michael appeared before a court in Varna to appeal against his sentence. In November the court rejected his plea. That month, the family, together with Louise Ellman, delivered a 70,000-strong petition demanding justice for Michael Shields, to Downing Street. In March 2006 an appeal was heard in the Supreme Court in Sofia. The court reduced the sentence from fifteen years to ten. However, they refused to grant a retrial, which would have enabled a warrant to be issued for Graham Sankey. In October, the Foreign Office confirmed that Michael could serve out the rest of his sentence in the UK. Even then, the Bulgarian authorities refused to release him to a UK prison until compensation of £90,000 was paid. Liverpool raised the money in a series of public events. In November, Michael arrived in the UK to serve the remainder of his sentence.

A year later, the Bulgarian government announced it was up to the British government to pardon him. Jack Straw was now Minister of Justice and his Ministry responded that pardons could only be granted where the case could not be referred to an appellate court, and where new evidence shows the individual concerned did not commit the offence.

The British campaign was reinvigorated. Ellman used Parliamentary privilege to name Graham Sankey as the man who launched the assault and claimed an abundance of new witness evidence. The British courts began to clear a way for Michael's case to be reviewed by Jack Straw. In October 2008, Michael won the right to a judicial review of his case. Two months later the case was heard and two senior judges ruled that the Justice Secretary did have the 'power and jurisdiction' to exercise the ancient Royal prerogative of mercy in his case. The Merseyside police investigated the facts at Jack Straw's request, but in July he provisionally refused the application for a pardon. This caused a public outcry in Liverpool. Jack Straw met Shields' parents at Blackburn town hall on 28th August and it would appear that much of the original evidence had not filtered through to him.

'At this meeting, following a series of questions which I put to the family, I was told for the first time about a visit by two members of the Shields family to the home of a man alleged to be responsible for the crime for which Michael Shields was jailed,' Straw's statement said. 'I was told that, in the course of the visit, that man made an oral confession to the crime in front of several other people. This episode, I was told, happened on 22nd July, 2005, a day after the start of Mr Shields' trial in Bulgaria.'

Straw caused further inquiries to be made. Two weeks later, Michael was pardoned and released into the arms of his jubilant family. He had spent four years in Bulgarian and British prisons. No action has ever been taken against Sankey.

My part in the British campaign was a modest one. I supplied statements of what happened in court on demand to the various lawyers who had taken up Michael's case in the UK. I am sure in my own mind that Jack Straw was convinced of Michael's innocence from the outset. It was a question of collecting overt evidence to support his personal opinion.

In February 2013, I travelled to Liverpool Lime Street station to have lunch with Michael Shields. To my surprise, I was met by his father, Michael Shields senior, whom I'd last seen in 2005. Michael's book *Michael Shields, My Story*, had been written with the aid of Greg O'Keeffe, a local journalist who followed the story, and had recently been published. I was very happy to interview the father whilst waiting for his son.

The father had turned up at the station with a friend of his, a local taxi driver. I was introduced to the friend as 'someone who had helped with the campaign behind the scenes'. Evidently, any help received from outside Liverpool didn't really rate. They took me to the father's home, a recently decorated, smart, rented flat in the heart of Liverpool. The taxi left. I was invited to choose between the parlour and the kitchen and chose the kitchen. We didn't have lunch, but I was plied with endless cups of tea. We both expected Michael Jr. to turn up later. He was an apprentice electrician and travelled all over the UK. Unknown to his father he was actually in Blackpool (about an hour's drive away) and so I wasn't able to stay to see him.

There is a paragraph in Michael's book that says that his parents were so busy campaigning that they both lost their jobs whilst he was in prison. His mother had indeed lost her job. Through the stress of worry over Michael she was unable to turn up for work and after about twelve months she was dismissed. Michael senior had built up a prosperous window cleaning business over the years. He was self-employed and luckily his customers remained loyal to him. Michael's mother still hadn't recovered and talked about Michael's experience every day. She still felt the need to get in touch with Michael frequently.

His father told me: 'We see him about twice a week. He's buying his own flat with a lovely girlfriend, who is a teacher, and life is going very well for him. Sometimes Michael works away in Scotland or London but his mother is constantly phoning him because she needs reassurance whenever he's away. We've learnt to cope as best we can.'

Immediately after a bail application, very early in the case, Michael was returned to jail and spoke to an English-speaking Bulgarian in his cell. They got talking about the differences between Bulgaria and England and he was told: 'Money rules in Bulgaria. Money is number one. If you pay the person who gets hurt, then you go home.' Until I'd read the book and came across this quote, I hadn't realised that we had been dealing with an officially-sanctioned ransom demand all along.

It was very hard for the Shields family to understand Jack Straw's dilemma. They thought he should have apologised for keeping Michael in prison in the UK for two years. Jack Straw had not only agreed with me at the time that Michael was probably innocent, but shortly afterwards he contacted Joe Anderson (the kingpin of the campaign to free Michael) and told him that he believed Michael was innocent, but that his hands were tied.

13

A Tale of Two Nannies

One of them was a teenager working as an au pair in Boston, the other a middle-aged registered child minder in California. Louise Woodward was one of the most sensational cases I was ever involved in and certainly ranks with the plane spotters' case in Greece. In 2007, she was named the 'most notorious criminal convicted in Massachusetts' by Boston law magazine *Exhibit A*. On the other hand, the Manjit Basuta case created little interest, either in the United States or in Britain. Both women were convicted of homicide and sentenced to twenty years and twenty-five years respectively.

Massachusetts: Louise Woodward

On 4th February, 1997 an alarm call was received by the emergency services in Newton, Massachusetts. A British au pair, Louise Woodward, reported that Matthew, the younger son of her employers Mr and Mrs Eappen, was in distress. Within twenty-four hours of the contact with emergency services, Louise was arrested and charged with battery. Five days later, when the baby died, the charge moved to one of first-degree murder.

Louise's mother, Sue Woodward, contacted me within days of the arrest and asked me to act as the parents' representative in the UK, liaising with the American lawyers for public relations purposes. I remember assuring her that if one had to be tried overseas, the criminal courts of Massachusetts were as good as anywhere – and anyway, didn't we speak the same language? Then I watched with horror as a perfect legal storm engulfed the hapless teenager.

I had rather forgotten that Massachusetts has its own dark history, such as the witches of Salem and the pro-Irish/anti-British origins of Boston (always a major source of clandestine IRA funding). They were also good at miscarriages of justice for foreigners. I had a ringside seat.

The first problem Louise faced was the first Amendment to the American Constitution: the freedom of the press to speculate widely in pending cases. An extraordinary hate campaign inspired by both prosecution and the Eappen family against Louise had its effect. As a result, just before the trial opened a poll in Boston showed that more than eighty-five per cent of the public had already made up their minds that Louise was guilty. In other words, the pool from which the jury was to be drawn had already been poisoned against her. A motion to change the venue of trial was denied and I'm firmly of the opinion that the extraordinary result of the trial began with that decision.

The discrimination shown against Louise in the pre-trial phase resulted in her remaining in prison instead of on bail. The prosecutor admitted that he had framed the charges at the urging of the Eappen family. The first-degree murder charge was not a decision he would have been likely to come to if Louise had been a member of a prominent local family with good community ties.

The prosecution case was that the baby had been violently shaken and thrown on the floor on 4th February, causing injuries to the baby's central nervous system – 'shaken baby syndrome' – and, separately, a fractured skull. These injuries could only have been caused by Louise Woodward, since there was no one else in the house at the time.

The defence case was essentially that the skull injury was 'old' – about two weeks old – and could have been caused by anyone in the Eappen family or others who had access to the child. The pressure causing the symptoms of shaken baby syndrome was due to the dislodging of a blood clot forming after the original skull fracture.

The whole argument was technical and the principal evidence consisted of sixteen assorted medical experts. Almost all the prosecution experts were local and some of them colleagues of the Eappens.

The trial was impeccably conducted until the jury retired to consider their verdict. They then spent three days in their deliberations during which they returned to the judge on a number of occasions. In particular, after deliberating for two days, they returned asking to review the medical evidence. They were given only the prosecution evidence and repeatedly refused that of the defence. Further, they were effectively bullied by the judge into returning a verdict without this key evidence, even after their foreman stressed for a second time that it was of paramount importance they see the defence evidence. The lawyers were ashen-faced and Louise was hysterical when the jury returned a verdict of guilty of murder.

The judge's behaviour in dealing with the jury was the most spectacular breach of the principle of parity of arms between prosecution and defence – the duty to be even handed – that I have ever witnessed in a country with a mature justice system. It was, in the circumstances, a direction to convict. The conundrum was what made a reputable and experienced American judge behave in such a monstrously unjust manner. I am sure it was actually a Herculean attempt to make the jury system work quickly to the obvious conclusion: an acquittal. Tragically, the detailed complexity of the medical evidence confused the jury and made such an attempt self defeating. Judge Zobel had achieved the worst possible result with the very best intentions.

It was at this stage that I stopped being a concerned outsider keeping British public opinion favourable by commentating on the trial for the media and appearing on chat shows. I had been generally concentrating on the many other things I was doing at the time. What could go wrong?, I had thought. For me it had turned, in some ways, into a reprise of the Karyn Smith case, a young woman who was the victim of an intolerable injustice. But in other ways it was a totally different situation; on the surface Louise had had the best defence, but what was troubling me in particular was a 'noose or loose' defence choice allowed in Massachusetts. The defendant could force the jury to decide between murder and acquittal, leaving out the normal option of manslaughter. Louise may have nominally chosen the disastrous option, but in fact it was chosen by her clever defence lawyers to put pressure on the jury – and she was the one to suffer the consequences. I plunged myself into a unique crusade to change public opinion not here in Britain but in Boston, Massachusetts.

That night I wrote a passionate letter to the *Boston Globe*. It took me about thirty minutes. I didn't even think about it, but faxed it straight to the paper. It appeared on the day of the sentencing. I still think it's one of the best letters I have ever written.

LETTERS TO THE EDITOR

I am a British lawyer with over thirty years' experience. When Gary and Sue Woodward came to us for advice concerning Louise after her arrest, I publicly proclaimed that if one had to be tried outside one's native land there would be few places one would prefer to the Commonwealth of Massachusetts.

I, like many others on both sides of the Atlantic, watched with growing disbelief and horror as accumulative human errors produced a catastrophic miscarriage of justice and blatant abuse of human rights by an experienced and reputable trial judge.

Two substantial points in this trial attract immediate attention.

– The extraordinary local gamble of 'loose or noose', where an inexperienced foreign youngster is encouraged to bet her life on the advice of respected lawyers, including the active encouragement of the trial judge. In effect the lawyers were the gamblers and she was merely the stake.

– Second, when the jury have been out a long time and return to review the key medical evidence, they are given the prosecution evidence, repeatedly refused parallel defence evidence, and bullied by the judge into returning a verdict without it. It was the most spectacular display of breach of that most fundamental principle of fair trials, parity of arms between prosecution and defence that I have ever witnessed in a country with a mature justice system.

Justice is always a human activity prone to error even in the best legal systems. One of the characteristics of the great common law tradition is that when serious mistakes are made those in authority strive to rectify the position without delay. Now the trial judge has both the power and opportunity to show that he is both human and personally in that great tradition.

STEPHEN JAKOBI, *Director, The Fair Trials Abroad Trust, Richmond, England.*

I was informed it had some effect, even in Boston. The American media had changed sides with the verdict and were now all for an involuntary manslaughter compromise. In the Commonwealth of Massachusetts and four other states of the USA, the trial judge has powers to reject or modify the verdict of the jury. Two working days after the verdict, the defence asked him to use these powers and the prosecution demanded he leave the verdict as it stood. Judge Zobel took time out for reflection.

During this recess I was invited onto *Newsnight* to gaze into a crystal ball and predict the result. Everything in court had been televised across the world. I'd watched the whole trial as a commentator for Sky television and in particular the judge's face when the jury delivered its verdict. When I understood the power to change the verdict in Massachusetts, I was convinced the verdict wouldn't stand.

Outside the make-up room in BBC Television Centre presenter Kirsty Wark was discussing what I might say as we were waiting to come on air. I predicted the judge would do something spectacular.

'You mean as we talk, she might be on a plane back home?' she asked me.

'I suppose there is an outside chance that that would happen,' I replied.

'Would you be willing to come on and say that on air?' she asked me. I wasn't willing to go as far as that, but I said I was confident that the verdict of the jury would not stand and stuck to it in interview.

The next day, Judge Zobel reduced the conviction to involuntary manslaughter and sentenced Louise to time served, allowing her immediate release. In giving his explanation of what he thought happened, the judge adopted the defence argument – that Louise may have been a little rough and dislodged a blood clot from the old skull injury – in its entirety. Sometime after the case was over he said his main regret about the trial was that he had refused to allow Mrs Eappen's extraordinary attempt to pervert the course of justice to be shown to the jury: she had taken a video of her attempt to get Matthew's two-year-old brother to say Louise had harmed the baby. The brother constantly told his mother, 'Louise loved both me and Matthew'.

I never doubted that Louise was innocent of murder or any intention to harm the child. It was her explanation of what had happened that convinced me. If an accident had happened to the child, she would have told the police. If deliberate harm had been done to the child, she would have said the same thing. Louise said that nothing had happened to the child. That caused consternation to the defence team, who tried to make her admit an accident might have happened since it would make defending her easier, but she was adamant.

Trawling through the dense mass of scientific evidence, one uncontradicted fact produced by the defence should have concluded the case. Osteoblasts – specialised cells produced in the bone marrow for knitting bone fractures – were present at the site of the fracture. They would have taken at least nine days to arrive at the fracture site in the skull. The theory of the old skull fracture had been scientifically proved.

So who had been responsible for Matthew's death? One of the most intriguing pieces of evidence produced at trial was that Matthew had suffered a fracture of the wrist about three weeks before his death, which was discovered during the post-mortem. And one of the major unanswered questions is not only who caused it, but why both parents – experienced doctors – were completely unaware of it. It seems likely that the wrist and skull injury occurred at the same time.

All the evidence points to an unnoticed accident having occurred around early/mid January with four possible perpetrators: Mr or Mrs Eappen; Louise; or the two-year-old elder brother during play.

The defence team found evidence from a third party that the older brother was jealous of the baby, but the evidence wasn't used since they were of the opinion that it would not look good to the jury.

I had got my personal reading of the prospects for the case entirely wrong from start to finish in that first telephone call with Louise's mother. Even the opinion on the common language was wrong. Louise's explanation of changing the baby's nappy had included the expression 'I popped the baby on the bed'. It was misunderstood by the police officer involved as having 'dropped' the baby on the bed, since the use of the word 'popped' was unknown in Boston.

But the melodrama was not yet over. The prosecution appealed and Louise was marooned in Massachusetts for several months until their appeal could be heard.

The winter and spring of 1998 was a busy period for FTA. The Woodward case was now in limbo so far as I was concerned. The Phil Cornish trial was an extra burden and I made my trips to Romania and Vienna at this time. We were also in deep financial trouble due to delayed payment of EU funds. The bank overdraft had reached crisis proportions: my house was at risk and I was on the point of taking out a new mortgage.

Louise's American lawyers kept me informed and sent me all the legal pleadings relating to the appeal as they accumulated, but I was a totally passive spectator. Through televised debates with noted American academics I realised how difficult it was in practice to overturn a jury's verdict, however unsound, and there was a real danger that the prosecution would succeed at the hearing. I was very frustrated.

Meanwhile, an Internet support group had formed with its own website: louisewoodwardboston.com. Largely local young professionals with a sprinkling of lawyers, they were concerned, as I was, about what would happen if the appeal went 'pear shaped'. I had joined the chat room (the Internet on-line discussion group) under the grandiloquent pseudonym of 'Justice' and was trying to keep the group both constructive and sane.

Enter nutcase Texas lawyer Daniel J Shea with a Blackadder-type 'cunning plan'. He would take over the Louise Woodward case without instructions from Louise and had cooked up details of a monstrous conspiracy he was convinced existed. His theory was along the lines that Louise's lawyers, including me, had entered into a conspiracy to get Louise convicted and therefore protect the insurance company paying for her defence from an action for damages by the Eappens. He announced his intention to sue me, not the American lawyers. I suppose he thought I was the weakest link and a foreigner to boot, so that I would be compelled to give details and documents that were supposedly in my possession and uncover the conspiracy. He was going to sue me for libel in the hope of getting me before a Texas Jury with his objective in mind.

The other members of the group were frightened he would damage the cause by his actions. A plethora of hostile emails filled the chat room. A fellow Texan was of the opinion he was up to the old Texas pastime of 'throwing Buffalo chips' – bullshit!

I dismissed it as a Texas lawyer's joke until I eventually received a Texas district court summons, suing me for $100 million libel damages in my capacity as 'director of corporate membership' of the Fair Trials Abroad Trust.

I did some online research and got the help of one of the young Boston lawyers who had joined the support group. I sent a short letter to the presiding Texas judge, in which I made the observation that it was possible for the court, using its own initiative, to review any case that may be frivolous, vexatious or an abuse of process. The judge must have agreed with me on at least one of those grounds because I heard no more about it.

On the 16th June, 1998, the Appeal Court affirmed the guilty verdict by a seven-nil vote but in a close, four-three split decision the court rejected the prosecution's appeal against the reduction of the conviction to involuntary manslaughter and Louise was free to go home. I had got so involved that I was euphoric for days.

Louise was a special guest at our charitable status celebrations in

2000. A small group photograph including her and I appeared on the front page of *The Times* the following morning.

California: Manjit Basuta

Manjit Basuta had nothing going for her when her troubles began. She was a rather severe-looking 43-year-old Asian woman who'd lived in the United States for ten years. She had been running a day care service for toddlers from her home in San Diego, California, where she lived because of her husband's job as an IT executive. On March 17th, 1998, one of the six children in her care, thirteen-month-old Oliver Smith, collapsed and died. Manjit tried desperately to revive him while her Guatemalan assistant, Cristina Carrillo, called the emergency services. The coroner's office decided that Oliver had died of shaken baby syndrome as a result of ill treatment by an adult. At first Cristina backed up her employer's story that Oliver had been pushed by another child or fallen over. Then after three days she abruptly switched to an allegation that Manjit had shaken the toddler in a blind rage until he passed out because he would not come to her to have his nappy changed. She was to change her version of events a total of ten times more before the end of the trial. The prosecution told the jury that she had given the original version because Manjit had threatened to report her as an illegal immigrant. Whatever the truth of that argument, Cristina has to go down in history as one of the most unreliable witnesses to be produced in any court.

Manjit had always pleaded her innocence. Her defence team claimed that Carrillo's evidence had been changed so often as to make it meaningless. They argued that there was no evidence against their client and suggested that Oliver had had an injury some months previously, and had then suffered 'spontaneous rebleeding', which could have been easily and unintentionally caused. It was the Louise Woodward defence, but backed up not only with expert medical and scientific evidence but also by physical facts. This child was not six months old but thirteen months old. He weighed twice as much as Matthew Eappen – well over ten kilos. Most of us have lugged around ten kilo bags of one sort or another; try shaking such a bag violently, as violently as might cause internal brain damage.

This baby created a record as the heaviest and oldest baby where an accused was convicted of causing shaken baby syndrome. The defence team had not only lined up expert evidence on the cause of the injury, they also had a mechanical engineer who had conducted experiments on the difficulties of shaking ten kilos of dead weight, let alone a squirming active child.

There was also another crucial piece of evidence that pointed to causation. Audrey Amaral, the child's mother, had gone through a bitter divorce a few months previously in which her husband accused her of abusing the boy. The defence was in a much stronger position than the defenders of Louise Woodward.

Journalists talk loosely about the American system of criminal justice. One might as well talk about the criminal justice system of Great Britain. In fact we have three: England and Wales; Scotland; and Northern Ireland. In the United States the criminal justice systems differ from state to state. There are therefore more than fifty criminal justice systems in the United States, including the Federal justice system. In Massachusetts district judges are appointed for life. In California they are elected, and judicial quality is not the main criterion. Manjit's trial judge was such a poor judge that all the defence evidence I have outlined above was excluded from the trial. He wouldn't allow the defendants to call their experts or to cross-examine Mrs Amaral.

When a California jury convicted Manjit on Monday, 14th June, 1999, a lot was made by commentators – including me – about racial prejudice against Asian immigrants. We thought it was the key factor. Re-examining evidence that the jury was allowed to hear, I am no longer so sure. The defence had been shut out of the case by judicial incompetence and the jury had only heard the sound of one hand clapping, that of the prosecutor.

A new act had been passed by the California state legislators

142

providing for a mandatory minimum sentence of twenty-five years for causing the death of a child under the age of eight. Manjit's case was the first to be tried under the new legislation. In August 1998, whilst I was on holiday, Judge William H Kennedy held back from handing down this mandatory sentence and suggested that twenty-five years for an unpremeditated crime might constitute cruel or unusual punishment. He asked the lawyers in the case to formulate their arguments on the point for his consideration in early October.

When October came, he decided that since Manjit had lied on her immigration form she was obviously of such bad character that he had no alternative but to sentence her to the full twenty-five years. One might speculate as to what his reaction would have been if he had been an appointed judge, rather than a judge standing for re-election. His Pontius Pilate moment of conscience had passed and being compassionate to illegal Asian immigrants was not going to endear him to his electorate.

I knew nothing about this case until June 1998, when I was approached by Amelia Gentleman, a *Guardian* reporter, who was writing an article on the case with my old collaborator Duncan Campbell. Based on what I was told, it was obvious to me that this was a case where racial discrimination was the major factor and I was quoted as saying so. It was only as a result of the article that the family approached me to assist them and I was put in contact with the defence lawyer, Eugene Airedale. I was then able to appreciate just how badly his case had been butchered by decisions of the trial judge. We did the best we could, with Sarah heavily involved, to counter the institutionalised commercial racism in the tabloids. Manjit was supported by *The Guardian*, the *Daily Mirror* and her regional local paper, the *Ascot Gazette*, where a journalist had doggedly reported every twist and turn of Manjit's ordeal from the very beginning.

While the dramatic sentencing developments unfolded, I was away on holiday. *The Independent* featured an article by Andrew Gumbel, which not only suggested that I was making intemperate statements about the iniquities of US courts but that I had lost sight of the fact that nobody on either side of the Atlantic, including Mrs Basuta's lawyers, had seriously suggested that she was denied a fair trial. Since the article was written in the interval between the announcement of the possibility of cruel and unusual punishment and its dramatic conclusion, we were all keeping quiet and hoping for a favourable outcome. I wonder how Gumbel felt when, after the decision to send Manjit to prison, the appeal court had no difficulty in ordering a retrial. After three years imprisonment, Manjit was freed, 'time served', on a plea bargain.

It was Andrew Gumbel's article that produced a theory that arrogant mistakes in defence tactics caused the convictions of both Louise and Manjit: 'noose or loose' for Louise and a decision not to put Manjit in the witness box in the belief the defence had done enough. The real cause of both miscarriages of justice was bad judging: a mistake by a fine judge in Massachusetts and a simply awful display in California.

14

Nailing the Troublemakers

Large crowds always spell trouble for the police. The problem is the same, whether the crowd is drawn together for the purposes of a demonstration or for a football match. The vast majority of the participants are peaceful, law-abiding citizens but there are always the troublemakers – the direct action militants amongst the demonstrators and the hooligans in the pre-match crowd. Their purpose is essentially the same: to use the crowd as an excuse for violence.

A foreign element in the crowd, an international football match or a demonstration against an economic summit, makes life even more difficult for the local police. They know their own troublemakers but not the foreigners, and a form of institutional xenophobia often exacerbated by the local press seems to take over. It's a sort of reverse of the old Cockney Londoners' rallying cry – 'Here's a foreigner, heave a brick at him'. If someone heaves a brick at the police, it must have been a foreigner.

The police often charge into the unruly crowd and grab any bewildered innocents they can catch. The real troublemakers are prepared for the police charge and have already dropped their weapons and melted into the crowd. At the end of the rioting when the crowd has departed, the police have a collection of weapons on the one hand and a bunch of foreigners they have managed to grab on the other. The ensuing conspiracy is in the marriage between the weapons and the arrestees followed by charges relying solely on unsupported police statements.

Belgium: Mark Forrester

Belgium already had an unfortunate history of football violence before it became co-host to the 2000 European Championship. Disaster had occurred on 29th May, 1985, when escaping fans were pressed against a wall in the Heysel Stadium in Brussels before the start of the 1985 European Cup final between Juventus of Italy and Liverpool. Thirty-nine Juventus fans died and 600 were injured. The incident has its parallels with the Hillsborough disaster in Sheffield in 1989. The fans were blamed but the fundamental problem was the construction of the stadium and the separation of the rival supporters. The old Heysel stadium was never used for football again and the Belgians were determined that there should be no repeat. The Belgians co-hosted Euro 2000 and they expected mass arrests during the course of the interstate competition as a result of football fans rioting.

The Belgian Parliament produced a novel fast-track procedure for dealing with these 'hooligans.' The only offences triable were serious offences carrying at least a year's imprisonment. The trial had to start within five days and be over a week from arrest. Since this could not be done under Belgium's normal examining magistrate system, his powers were given to the prosecutor. As a result the prosecutor was to decide what evidence should be called for the hearing for both sides.

Parliamentarians warned the Belgian Government during the debate on the legislation that it was a deliberate defiance of the ECHR. Not only do the strict time limits contravene the rule that the defence must have adequate time to prepare, they must have the right to summon their own witnesses on the same terms as the prosecution.

Mark Forrester, a thirty-three-year-old family man from Birmingham, fell victim to this potentially toxic mixture of police conspiracy and abusive court procedure. He'd been a member of the England supporters club for some years and had a ticket for the England v. Germany match. He became one of the 400 Britons arrested in the centre of Brussels on June 16th. His party had been thrown out of a café, where they had been sheltering from a mob, because the proprietor had been instructed to close it, and they found themselves in the path of the riot police. The last thing any of the group saw of Mark was when he was singled out and thrown to the ground. Mark was arrested and accused of fomenting riots and assault on police officers.

His trial began within the five days. It was a classic case relying entirely on the unsupported evidence of police officers. A police officer based in a 'spotter' helicopter assisting the riot police stated he was absolutely sure that he had seen Mark start a riot in The Grand Place at 14.15 and kept it going every time the police looked as though they were gaining control. He said he saw Mark start another riot outside O'Reillys bar at 18.15 and again keep it going. He added Mark attacked five police officers from behind and disappeared into the crowd. It was the equivalent of the Holmesian curious incident of the dog in the night-time: the dog did nothing in the night-time and that was the curious incident. No evidence from any assaulted policeman was produced and the witnesses did not know their names. There were two strategically placed CCTV cameras but no video evidence was produced. An expert gave the weird excuse that the videos were taken for the purposes of crowd control and not identification. The 'expert' who produced the original excuse in court was, it transpires, the public relations officer of the Brussels' police service.

The defence was Mark's well-supported alibi for these alleged incidents. Mark was a member of a party of eight, including his father Carl. At 14.15 the party had yet to arrive in Brussels. At 18.15 the party had just logged into their hotel, finished unpacking, and when Mark was supposed to be assaulting police officers he was in the pub next door to the hotel eating an evening meal. There were statements in support from the hotel staff. Mark was convicted of assaulting police officers and sentenced to a year's imprisonment.

Between conviction and appeal I desperately tried to get hold of video evidence that our Belgian lawyer Jan Ferman (who was later to become a distinguished Fair Trials International trustee and allow us to use his premises as a temporary Brussels office), could produce before the appeal court re-hearing. The British police had sent a travelling squad to liaise with the Belgian police and it was fully equipped with hand-held video recording equipment. I discovered that there were in existence British recordings of the entire incident in front of the café. The British police were very frank about the incident off the record but said that due to international agreement they could only produce the evidence in their hands on the order of the foreign court or at the request of the Belgian police. I reported back to Jan, who told me in view of the conspiracy going on there was no chance of introducing it. The police, prosecution and judiciary would join together to suppress vital but procedurally inconvenient evidence. I attended the appeal, which we duly lost. We managed to avoid Mark's return to prison and his automatic inclusion in the British police hooligans list was cancelled, but that was a damage limitation exercise. Years later the Belgian constitutional court declared the law illegal.

Portugal: Garry Mann

Four years later, Portugal hosted the next European Championship. Forty-six-year-old Garry Mann, from Faversham, Kent, was the victim, this time along with eight others, of another textbook police cock-up in the handling of football-related violence.

The facts behind his arrest were almost a carbon copy of the Brussels incident down to a location outside a café and the mysterious disappearance of CCTV footage within twenty-four hours of the arrest. The hurried trial of the Albufeira nine had all the usual features of arguably the worst legal system in Europe, ranging from an overburdened defence lawyer with no time allowed to take instructions, through lack of interpretation to non-production of key evidence.

The British journalist and a travelling police officer present

148

reported the blatant xenophobic behaviour by the trial judge. The case before the nine was that of a Portuguese citizen charged out of the same incident. There were two police officers giving evidence, one officer more favourable to the defendant than the other. The magistrate announced that he was not willing to accept the second officer's evidence. He preferred the first officer's evidence and acquitted the native citizen. When it came to the turn of the British, only the second officer gave evidence against them. The magistrate convicted. The police evidence that he just rejected was good enough for the British scum!

The problem for Garry was that the huge skinhead looked the part of a football hooligan. Perhaps that was why he was arrested not when rioting but by plainclothes police on his way to his hotel in the early hours of the morning. He not only appeared a suitable scapegoat for the police but also for the magistrate, who sentenced him to two years' imprisonment when all the others received suspended sentences. *The Sun* joined in. Their headline: MORONS WHO HAVE SHAMED NATION had his photograph above it. Appearances were deceptive; the gallant fireman who had won a bravery award had had an exemplary record for a quarter of a century. The magistrate had ordered his immediate deportation and perhaps mistakenly the authorities deported him without imprisonment.

In the intervening couple of days before he was released, populist Home Secretary David Blunkett proved his credentials by vowing to 'nail' the hapless Garry in this country on his arrival.

One of our great columnists, Simon Jenkins, wrote this powerful article in *The Times*:

It goes without saying that a skinhead football supporter getting drunk in an Algarve pub at 3.30am does not arouse natural sympathy... For all I know he may be a serial football hooligan. No such claim was proved in court. Aged 46, with a family, a job, no previous conviction and an appeal pending, Mann seemed entitled to the benefit of legal doubt before his life was ruined by a prison sentence. The Home Secretary offered him none. A fanatical advocate of 'executive justice', Mr Blunkett rushed to a radio studio to demand that Mann get behind bars. He was 'working hard' to that end 'because I haven't given up on the idea that we are going to nail this individual'. Nail him to what, I wonder? To a prison door or a cross? Mann's appeal or subsequent trial in Britain is hopelessly prejudiced.'

By the time I met Garry just before the homecoming press conference he was on the verge of a breakdown. He was sure that the great and powerful in Britain were going to join forces with those terrifying Portuguese to destroy him, despite his tearful innocence. I managed, together with his British solicitor, to get him to face the press conference and he stumbled through a prepared statement. It was as clear to the more responsible assembled press as it was to me that he was really in no fit state to answer questions.

Within twenty-four hours of the British consternation with the trial going public, the Portuguese college of judges issued a press statement of complete solidarity with the trial judge. Since all the judges had already prejudged any issues we might raise on appeal, we went through the motions of their appeal system simply in order to get to the European Court of Human Rights. We never got off the ground in the Portuguese system. We couldn't find a local lawyer who would take on the case, we couldn't lodge papers in English. When we finally got an application filed with the European Court of Human Rights, it was refused at registrar level so the merits of Garry Mann's case were never reviewed by any judges abroad.

However, David Blunkett's nailing efforts seemed to have petered out. At home, there was an attempt to put the nine on the prohibited foreign travel list. The Home Office application was heard in the Uxbridge court and a British judge effectively ruled that the trial had been conducted so badly that it could not be used as a pretext for further penalties. That's where we thought the matter ended.

I was shocked four years later when a British solicitor telephoned me and told me that British police had arrested Garry at his home on a European Arrest Warrant issued by Portuguese authorities in 2008. When asked why it had taken so long for them to issue the Arrest Warrant, Portuguese authorities claimed to be unaware that Garry had not served a sentence in the UK.

In August 2009, senior district judge Timothy Workman, sitting at City of Westminster Magistrates' Court, ordered that he be sent to Portugal. It didn't help that his British lawyers missed a deadline to lodge a challenge by one day, meaning that he was unable to have a full appeal against the extradition. The British lawyers' mistake, so the court was told, followed an earlier error by Mr Mann's Portuguese legal team which also failed to file appeal documents, in his case within strict time limits (they never had a chance).

The presiding judge of the appellate court, Lord Justice Moses, said that Mr Mann was the victim of 'what appears to be a serious injustice. After a hearing condemned by a police officer as a "farce", he faces two years in prison, over five years since his original conviction,' he added. 'He wished, on two separate occasions, to exercise a right of appeal... Through no fault of his own, his lawyers failed to act, with the result that he has never had the opportunity, by way of appeal, to advance his case that he is being deprived of a fair hearing.'

The Judge concluded that he hoped the European Court of Human Rights, or the diplomatic authorities in either the UK or Portugal, 'can strive to achieve some measure of justice for Mr Mann, a justice which he has been so signally deprived by those on whom he had previously relied'. The 2003 Extradition Act left him powerless to intervene in Mr Mann's case.

Whatever diplomatic moves were made came to nothing and on 12th May, 2010, Garry was sent to a Portuguese jail. He spent a year there before being transferred to a UK prison and eventually released three months later.

Before 9/11, the decision in the District Court would have, in practice, been allowed to stand and Garry would never have been ordered to return to Portugal. The European Arrest Warrant and its implementation under British law stripped him of his rights. This is a textbook example of the problems with the Warrant, however desirable the Warrant was, and is, in principle.

Italy: G8

It began for me with a telephone call to my home early on the morning of Sunday, 22nd July, 2001, from an anxious mother, and the telephone scarcely stopped ringing for forty-eight hours. That was my introduction to the worst abuse of police power in Europe of modern times.

The authorities were expecting trouble at the G8 summit in Genoa that had taken place the previous day. A notorious band of militant anarchists called the Black Bloc had announced well in advance that they were going to come out fighting in the accompanying demonstration. The flood of phone calls was because a midnight raid on a school had resulted in the arrest of more than ninety Spanish, German and British protestors. They had been denied Consular access until the following Tuesday or, in some cases, Wednesday. Italian demonstrators taken into custody at the same time were released the next day without charge.

To make matters worse for the anxious relatives, a high proportion of the British were in prison hospitals. They were recovering from injuries sustained during the raid on the Diaz Pertini school building, where ninety-three young demonstrators were bedding down on the floor for the night. In fact, the school had been selected by the local council as an overnight crash pad and communications centre for journalists and authorised peaceful demonstration groups. At least 150 armed riot police swarmed through the building, dispensing 'baton justice', resulting in damaged spines, broken ribs and cracked skulls. There were graphic accounts of pregnant women being deliberately beaten senseless. This was not the usual mess: it was the civil equivalent of My Lai, one of the most infamous events of the Vietnam War.

On the Sunday there was a farcical attempt at a cover-up. Senior officers held a press conference at which they announced that everybody in the building would be charged with aggressive resistance to arrest and conspiracy to cause destruction. They displayed the 'confiscated weaponry', which they presented as offensive weapons; it included seventeen cameras, thirteen pairs of swimming goggles, ten penknives – and a bottle of sun-tan lotion. By the middle of the week, at the first proper hearing for the victims of this police savagery, the state prosecutor described the charges as grotesque and the examining magistrate decided that all the arrests had been illegal. Those that were fit to travel were on their way home and my part in the matter was over. The various victims had their own British solicitors.

The affair of the Genoa G8 summit punishment squad rumbled on. The examining magistrate uncovered a horrific tale of organised, merciless savagery. The limp-wristed retribution took seven years to catch up with those who were responsible for more ill-treatment at Bolzaneto detention centre when the detained arrived there after the raid. It was described by public prosecutors as torture. Nick Davies of *The Guardian* gave a graphic description of what happened to them:

On arrival, they were marked with felt-tip crosses on each cheek, and many were forced to walk between two parallel lines of officers who kicked and beat them. Most were herded into large cells, holding up to 30 people. Here, they were forced to stand for long periods, facing the wall with their hands up high and their legs spread. Those who failed to hold the position were shouted at, slapped and beaten. One had an artificial leg and, unable to hold the stress position, collapsed.

Ester Percivati, a young Turkish woman, recalled guards calling her a whore as she was marched to the toilet, where a woman officer forced her head down into the bowl and a male jeered, 'Nice arse! Would you like a truncheon up it?' Several women reported threats of rape.

In July 2008, thirteen Italian *Carabineri*, GOMPI Mobile (Italian armed response police) and prison police were convicted for abuse of authority, abuse of office and uniform. Two medical staff were also convicted.

In November 2008 the raid trial concluded and thirteen police officers were convicted of their various crimes including Vincenzo Canterini (four years), the commander of the 7th Mobile unit.

None of them actually served prison terms. Their convictions and sentences were wiped out by a statute of limitations in 2009 before the appeals were heard and the politicians who were responsible for the whole affair were never put before the court.

Greece: Simon Chapman

A year later it was the turn of the Greeks. An EU economic summit was held in June 2003 at Thessalonica, Greece's second city. It was accompanied by the traditional anti-globalisation demonstration that could be expected in such affairs, and, as ever, the demonstration turned into a riot. Our client, Simon Chapman, then a thirty-year-old designer, from Basildon, Essex, was one of the twenty-nine protesters arrested. They were refused provisional liberty by the Greek courts on the grounds that they were all charged with such serious offences as continuous possession and use of explosives (Molotov cocktails), grievous harm, grievously resisting the police and rebellion against the state. The only evidence against the detainees was contained in the black backpacks allegedly found with them. Most were later freed, but Simon was detained, along with two Spaniards, a Syrian and a Greek, for allegedly possessing firebombs.

Everyone was expecting trouble, including the Greek television channels that were recording just about everything. As the remand hearings rumbled on, video evidence presented to the court clearly showed an astonishing metamorphosis: Chapman's bag changing from a blue rucksack when he was arrested to the black bag which contained the petrol bombs.

Unfortunately for Simon and the others who continued to be incarcerated, they were in Greece, not Italy. The judges repeatedly refused to look at this evidence for months, and several appeals for release on bail were refused. It took major pressure from the European institutions and a seven-week hunger strike that nearly resulted in Simon's death before he was released the following year.

15

The Canaries

The Canary Islands are a law unto themselves and Tenerife has a particularly bad reputation. In 2002, two cases arrived on my desk within a few months of each other. Both of them concerned young Britons in their twenties, one male, the other female.

Kevan Sloan's case started off as one of mistaken identity. It was based entirely on a single, shaky piece of evidence, and the whole incident turned into a ferocious exhibition of xenophobia directed at the expat community in Tenerife. He was at all times on my watch in prison in Tenerife. I never met him and Sarah and I mainly worked on his case abroad.

Terry Daniels' ordeal started five years before Kevan's and was based on guilt by association in the teeth of the presumption of innocence. Terry was in the UK when she came to us and I met her a number of times until she was extradited.

I discussed Kevan's case in Madrid with a Spanish Minister. On a subsequent visit to Brussels, I also spoke to two Spanish MEPs about the case, one of whom actually represented the Canary Islands. They all told me the same thing: 'Don't expect justice in the Canary Islands'. In their opinion, the entire system was corrupt and they advised me to go for an appeal in Madrid. From that time on I always viewed Tenerife as an island where trials are so unfair that even the other Spaniards notice.

Tenerife: Kevan Sloan

Kevan Sloan's mother, Eileen Forrester, contacted me shortly after his first trial had gone wrong. She was on a visit to the United Kingdom from the island of Tenerife, where she had settled and worked as a travel agent. On 19th March, 2002, we issued our first memorandum and summarised the case.

Kevan Sloan, age 26, from Kirkby, Liverpool has a shaven scalp, is 1.8 metres tall and of normal build. He has no criminal record and is highly valued by his builders' merchant employers where he has worked for the past 10 years and who are assisting him with his defence. He went on holiday to Tenerife with his uncle and aunt on the 11th May, 2001 and stayed with his mother who has a flat and works on the island as a travel agent. A few days later, on the 24th May, he was arrested and charged with a series of robberies that had apparently been committed by a man with dark curly hair, nearly a foot shorter (approx 20 cm), of between 30-35 years of age, of stout build and a native Spanish speaker.

Mr Sloan remained in prison awaiting trial, bail having been refused three times. At the commencement of the trial on 20th December 2001 in Santa Cruz he was offered a deal: Time served if he pleaded guilty. Mr Sloan refused. At the conclusion of the trial on Friday, the 18th January 2002, Mr Sloan was acquitted on 3 counts of robbery and found guilty on the fourth count of robbery for which he was sentenced to three and a half years imprisonment. On appeal to the Provincial Criminal Courts in Santa Cruz de Tenerife on the 8th of March 2002 the conviction was upheld.

The charges related to a series of five robberies that took place on minimarkets between February and May 2001. In general, the witnesses and the CCTV evidence agreed the robber to be fat, short and over thirty. There was one witness to one of the robberies who originally agreed with the other witnesses that CCTV gave a good likeness of her assailant. She changed her mind at a police line-up. Her evidence led to the conviction.

All the witnesses agreed that the robber spoke mother-tongue Spanish. The judge states in her judgment that there is no evidence that Kevan spoke Spanish. On Kevan's behalf there was evidence of good character from his employer and others and alibi evidence for all the incidents.

The real problem was the judge's xenophobia. All British ex-pats were asked how long they lived on the island and why they did not speak fluent Spanish. Employer's evidence was viewed with the remark that pay sheets and logs could have been faked. The judge remarked that Mr Sloan seemed disinterested in his fate. Since no interpretation was provided for him, except for his own evidence, he was unable to follow proceedings. As he could not effectively participate in his own trial, he could not possibly have any idea what his fate might be.

The defence lawyer's concluding argument was interrupted by the Judge and cut short after only twenty minutes.

On 8th March, 2002, the Provincial Criminal Court confirmed the original conviction and adopted the legal reasoning.

From an interview with the *Liverpool Echo:*

Kevan was jailed in 2001 for a series of bank robberies in Tenerife – despite witnesses claiming he was nowhere near the scene of any of the crimes when they took place... Even the intervention of human rights organisation Fair Trials Abroad and top level meetings between the then Home Secretary and his Spanish counterparts could not secure Kevan's release. The one thing that would have allowed Kevan to walk free from his prison cell was the one thing he was not prepared to do – admit guilt... But his principled stance meant he had to serve his full term in a jail where he was viewed with suspicion just for being English.

'It was an absolute nightmare,' he said. 'From the minute I went to jail I knew I was an outsider. I looked differently to most of the other inmates, acted differently and spoke differently. The worst thing about it was when I was in my cell, because none of the lads spoke English. We couldn't build up any kind of relationship or even have a laugh and a joke. It was tense all the time.'

Ironically, the first prison Kevan was sent to was in a place the Spanish call Hope. But the grinding regime at the Centro Penitenciario Tenerife 2 jail was almost enough to break Kevan. He said: 'There was no segregation at all. There were murderers, rapists and paedophiles. Everyone knew who they were and every time I saw them it just made me sick.

'I would see them walking about, sharing the same washroom as me and eating the same food and it made me realise just what a nightmare I had walked into. I knew that people were doing their best to get me out but whenever I felt down and looked at the mess I was in it made me feel like giving up...

'When you are as isolated as I was you cling onto every little thing that is important to you. I was in a jail in the north of the island, which was around 100 miles away from where my mum was living in Los Cristianos, but she still made the trip to visit me every weekend. When she came she always brought me all the English papers from the past week so I would have something to do to pass the time away. It is little things like that that got me through, especially when I was at my lowest....'

Tenerife: Teresa 'Terry' Daniels

On Monday, 2nd June, 2003 I was contacted early in the morning by a distressed mother, whose daughter was suffering from the effects of a near fatal brain haemorrhage. Pat Daniels had just been visited by three police officers armed with an international arrest warrant for her daughter, Terry. Terry didn't live at home, so Pat contacted her and she turned up at her mother's house to be arrested.

In the meantime, I arranged for Terry to be represented by the solicitors Bindmans. She was bailed later that day from Bow Street Magistrates' Court. We had received the utmost cooperation by extremely sympathetic police.

Shortly afterwards, we all had a meeting over tea on the terrace of the House of Commons with their energetic Member of Parliament. He had a complete grasp of the very tangled tale that the Daniels had to tell us, and he'd been working on the case for over three years. The most extraordinary thing was that Terry only discovered by accident that she was wanted in Spain. She applied for a police record for her job as a care assistant and found out that in fact her conviction for drug trafficking still stood. Even then her employer decided to keep her on, because her dedication and reliability had proved she could be trusted. I never met Terry before she was under medication. It was clear to me that here was a decent, honest young woman under great stress. Her mother Pat – the quintessential earth mother – came across as sturdy and full of common sense but obviously completely out of her depth.

Three years later, her MP gave an excellent summary of the case in the House of Commons:

Extract from Hansard, 18 January 2006

In the time available to me I should like briefly to summarise the chronological sequence of events in this case, and to comment on the trial appeals process.

On 12 June 1997, Teresa Daniels – hereinafter referred to as Terry – was arrested at Las Palmas airport in Tenerife in the company of her companion Antonio Benavides, who was in possession of 3.8 kg of cocaine. On 17 June, five days later, Terry was released on bail. Shortly afterward, she suffered a near fatal brain haemorrhage, but fortunately, as a result of early and effective medical intervention, she was saved and restored to health.

On 2 September 1997, Terry attended a court hearing that lasted 1½ hours, at which she was asked five questions and then told she was free to go. More than six months later, on 27 March 1998, Terry Daniels was sentenced to 10 years imprisonment for drug trafficking – precisely the same sentence as was imposed on her co-defendant Mr Benavides. He had previous criminal convictions, she did not. As I have mentioned, he had cocaine in his possession at the time of the arrest, she had none.

Terry's lawyer requested that she be given conditional liberty, which was granted to her. After a series of legal skirmishes, the first appeal by Terry's lawyers was heard on 12 November 1999. It was heard on the basis of written pleadings and dismissed in her absence. A copy of the judgement was never sent to her and a sentence of 10 years imprisonment was confirmed. In January 2000 Terry lodged a second appeal and in February 2000, she travelled to the United Kingdom to have a medical check-up. It transpired she needed to have a series of operations. In March 2000, in response to correspondence from me, the Spanish Ambassador sent me a letter with a report from the Spanish Directorate General of Penitentiary Institutions that stated that Terry had been released on 17 of June 1997.

In May 2002, more than two years later, an International Search and

Arrest Warrant was issued and in June 2003, a formal request for extradition was made. In August 2005, the Home Office – in the person of the Home Secretary... agreed to extradition and Terry was extradited in October 2005. Now she is in Topas prison in Salamanca, near Madrid. I said that I wanted to comment on the trial and the appeals process, and I shall do so in two very specific respects. One might be characterised as a comment on form and the other manifestly relates to substance. As far as the form is concerned, no translator was available during the trial. I must emphasise that, because I believe passionately that Terry has been ill-treated. Terry did not understand and therefore could not effectively participate in the proceedings. She didn't receive a copy of the judgement and yes, such was the level of misunderstanding and lack of information that she thought she was a witness at the hearing and not the defendant.

On the matter of substance, I make the point to the Minister of State that the evidence upon which Terry was convicted and sentenced was scanty indeed. I do not think I exaggerate when I say that it consisted overwhelmingly of the interpretation of an entry in her diary, which referred to an expected payment. The interpretation by the court put upon it was that she was recording an expectation of payment as a result of engagement in drug-trafficking. In fact, as she explained, she was referring to a payment that was to come to her as a result of a personal injury claim. The official translation of the contents of the diary was judged to be inadmissible, apparently on the grounds that it was out of time. It seems to me certain that Terry's human rights under the European Convention were breached in two respects: by the failure to admit the official translation of the diary, which would have lent weight to her pleading, and by the theft of her diary...

Terry met me on a drear November day in 2013 at Leighton Buzzard Station. In these situations I'm always scared I won't recognise the client after only a couple of meetings several years before. I needn't have worried. She was the only person left at the station entrance, since I'd blundered into the exit the other side of the station and was late. Terry was clearly a chain smoker. She smoked in the car and had to break off our interview to go outside for a cigarette. We drove a couple of miles down winding country lanes to a local pub where her mother Pat is the cook. The pub didn't look any different from when I lived nearby and had visited it in my first car nearly sixty years before. It must have been imagination, but it seemed the same bunch of regulars, all on Christian name terms. I was introduced all round – everyone knew about the interview – and we were then given a quiet corner. Terry chatted, full of nervous energy. She was a joy to record, with a good memory for incidents and chronological sequences.

I started by asking her how she coped, both during prison and afterwards. Her first concern was the brain aneurysm. The operation done in Tenerife before she was bailed in 1997 had not worked and she had it re-operated on in Britain. She'd been told by her British doctor, who confirmed it later to the court, that she was in constant danger of the aneurysm bursting under stress. She also suffered from depression, and she needed 24/7 medical attention.

'When I eventually returned to a Spanish prison I had some sort of medical assessment that required an English translator and the translator wasn't up to it,' she told me. As a result she nearly died.

In Salamanca, she said: 'They took me out for a scan on my head, but luckily someone at the last minute realised that I had a metal plate in my head and the machine could have done me a great deal of damage. I couldn't actually tell anybody about it. I was escorted by five, trigger-happy *guardia civils* and I was scared that if I tried to draw someone's attention they would interpret it as an escape attempt and either beat or shoot me. The rest of the medical attention was equally disgraceful but you just had to grin and bear it.

'That was true for everything. Any disruption you caused and they would make life unbearable for you... My first experience of seeing ill-treatment was when we arrived at the new prison and a German girl, probably suffering from schizophrenia or some sort of mental illness, made a fuss when she got off the bus. They thought she was just being obnoxious, so the prison guards took her away and beat her with truncheons. This was my first experience of the prison that I was likely to remain in for ten years and made me very frightened.'

Terry escaped ill-treatment from guards through behaving herself.

'I was beaten up by a fellow inmate once and witnessed quite a lot of violence around me,' she said.

However, she had a special circle of friends, the ETA girls (ETA is the Basque terrorist organisation). 'Not the hard-core, but the sympathisers – they were pretty innocent really. I don't know to this day why they looked after me – I guess it was some Irishman who suggested it. There was a close affinity between the IRA and ETA, so they took me under their wing.'

She learned a new Spanish phrase every day. 'Since I was the only British girl, I had to pick it up. It was television that helped me most – probably *The Simpsons,* because they talked English and the sub-titles were in Spanish. After about six or seven months, I was pretty good.'

When she returned to that same prison about eighteen months later, after repatriation, life was much better. She could not only speak the language, she could complete her own forms.

What was unique was her comparative experiences in women's prisons. She served nineteen months in Spain and another nineteen months in Britain on repatriation.

'In fact, the only thing that was easier about British prisons was the language. The other thing was that the visits were much easier for my mum when I was in Britain. It cost my mum a thousand pounds every time she came to visit me in Spain, but over here there was funding. But in Spain she needed money for such things as extra water and toilet rolls – and my fags; I could not give them up.'

She had the same complaints as Steve Toplass about food, but was shocked by the corruption.

'Any good food that was coming in was taken by the officers. I liked the Spanish tortilla and about once a fortnight we had chicken paella. Apart from that I lived on bread rolls. But at one point I did swell up quite badly because of all the rubbish that was going into me.'

When Terry got home she was affected by tinnitus (ringing in the ears). 'It was two years after I was released from prison when I finally got rid of it. It was driving me crackers.

'To tell the truth, prison is prison whether you're abroad or at home. You're still locked in and you still can't leave. Holloway was an experience in itself – it was like a madhouse. It was diabolical in Spain but then it's not very pleasant here, either. You still can't go out, you still can't go down to the shops and you still can't see your families when you want to.

When Terry came out she had so many problems she didn't know where to start. Normally in both Spain and Britain prisoners go through release in stages, such as home leave and voluntary work but she was abruptly turfed out.

It was several months before Terry could go outside without her mum. She was on parole for two-and-a-half years and only came off in April 2011. All the time she was under licence and a curfew, with conditions in residence and probation restrictions, she was frightened that she would be recalled or taken back. 'If you mess up, any slight thing you go back on a recall. Although I did everything by the book, the conditions were frightening because in there, you were protected. Once I was out, I was terrified that if I was in the wrong place at the wrong time, God knows what would happen.'

She is also stuck until 2019 with a prison record that prevents her getting work. 'I go in a queue, and ten people in the line in front of me have no criminal record. I haven't got a chance to explain what's gone on...'

Pat then joined us at the table and explained that she found the difficulties of visiting absolutely awful. She had been widowed and found a new partner, but that had caused problems.

'Terry suggested if we timed our visits for every other month we could go for three days and visit once a day,' she explained. 'We even got a Consular letter stating that Mickey was my common-law husband. They would let him in two days, but on the last day they would say *'no-no familia'*, meaning he wasn't one of the family.'

Going in and out was like going through airport security. 'At one time I was nearly down to my knickers, all the other times it was fine. It all depended who was in charge.'

The visit itself was a nightmare. 'We were locked in this little room with her,' remembered Pat. 'To begin with I saw her behind glass and that was the most horrendous thing because I couldn't even give her a cuddle. When Terry was moved to Britain life was a lot better and it was very much easier to visit. The guards, in particular at Cookham, were friendlier. I could take Terry's niece (one of my grandchildren). At security the guard said, "I'm very sorry, but we have to search the little girl." But they made it a sort of game for her so it was quite fun really. The second time she went to see Terry in prison, she marched into the room and spread her arms out like an old hand.'

Throughout this ordeal Terry's MP – John Bercow, now Speaker of the House of Commons – never gave up on her. When she arrived home, he procured an invitation to join him at one of the Queen's garden parties. One of their proudest possessions is a photograph of Pat and Terry standing next to him. They keep in touch.

Part 4:
External Relations

16

'To Comfort the Afflicted...' The Role of the Media

One of the great American 19th century columnists, Finley Peter Dunne, was the originator of the observation that a newspaper's function was 'to comfort the afflicted and afflict the comfortable'. There is no one more afflicted than an innocent in a foreign jail and no one more comfortable than a Foreign Office minister or mandarin. From the beginning, journalists were my natural allies and without them I am certain we could have accomplished very little. It followed that such successes as we had in forcing the Foreign Office and foreign governments to act depended upon the credibility and reputation for integrity that we acquired. My favourite way of launching a story was to write it myself and get it published in the legal section of *The Times*. That way, I not only set the story up for others to follow, I was also given an absolute control over the content. This was thanks to the good offices and support of the legal editor Frances Gibb, and our collaboration continued until I retired.

In the first year or two of FTA, I gathered a bunch of distinguished journalists from national TV and the press, who became 'the usual suspects': – the people I approached first with a good story if I couldn't write it myself.

Very early on the scene was Duncan Campbell, then the crime correspondent of *The Guardian*. We worked together on the lorry drivers' scandal and when he moved to the USA he introduced me to a number of the key cases from America, in particular, the Manjit

Basuta case referred to earlier. Robert Verkaik, then of *The Independent*, was a good friend to us and particularly reliable for European Union cases. But above all, Jon Silverman, then home correspondent of the BBC, was my mainstay for media advice. He became one of our trustees.

Without media support it would have been impossible for us to obtain any sort of justice for our clients, but in practice we were even more dependent on journalists then that. They turned out to be a major channel for obtaining clients. Every person arrested abroad has the right to contact their Consulate. But the policy of the British Consular service was to warn the prisoner and his family against publicity, leaving them with less reliable ways to find their way to us.

One of the ways they heard of us was via word-of-mouth from other prisoners. Later, they or their families would hear of us through media publicity about other cases. Local journalists would recommend us. Eventually, politicians consulted us about their constituents.

The most important source was the journalist covering the victim's home. Once we had acquired a general reputation it was usually the local journalist working on a new story that would telephone the Fair Trials number and ask for the 'Press Office'. Even when I was working alone we were generating enough publicity for the media to imagine we had a number of specialist staff.

This initial call turned into a form of triage. The journalist would tell me the facts of the story as he knew them from the first overseas report and a family interview. When I managed to find out all he had, I had to make an instant decision. The choices were:

1) 'Not one for us, I'm afraid' i.e. plainly guilty.

2) 'Here are a few points you might like to clear up; come back to me' i.e. I needed to know more before making up my own mind.

3) 'Yes I would be very interested to give you a statement or come on the programme. Please put the family in direct touch with me' i.e. plainly innocent. This was a rare one...

It was important to get the family to instruct me as quickly as possible. Of course it might take several months before we had anything in writing from the victim in a distant prison, but the next of kin in this country was acceptable.

If it was television there was a standard pattern for the initial story. It started with pictures of the victim followed by a thirty-second interview with a member of the victim's family, usually distressed. Then an interview with me: with luck, a thirty-second interview but all too often a two-second clip of me at my desk and a voice-over: 'Experts say it is a disgrace!' The programme would sometimes end with an interview with a junior government minister. Usually the presenter would read out a Foreign Office statement.

A lot of the interviews took place at my home. In media frenzy, the networks would shatter the calm of our quiet suburban backwater by descending on us wholesale, particularly if no one else was available during weekends or public holidays.

The Saudi nurses' case was a nightmare. Two British nurses, Deborah Parry and Lucy McLauchlan, were accused of murdering Yvonne Gilford, an Australian nurse working in the same hospital in Saudi Arabia. The case broke on the night of 23rd December, 1996. We were in the pre-mobile phone days. I had been in central London that day and returned late in the evening to find chaos. Competing teams from regional and national television were not only occupying both our study and the living room, but producers, presenters and crew were milling around in the kitchen. Other teams were waiting patiently in the drizzle outside. The telephone never stopped ringing. Sally manned the telephone whilst I gathered what was known about the cases and began to give interviews. I was halfway through my first with one of the major channels when Sally burst into the room. 'It's Jeremy Paxman on the phone and he wants you around right away to appear on *Newsnight*. They're sending a car.' So I wound up the interviews as quickly as I could and escaped to the waiting car.

The public in general, and my fellow lawyers in particular, had the idea that my life consisted of a great deal of luxurious travel to exotic locations to rescue Britons in distress. In fact, we couldn't even afford to pay me a salary. If there was to be any proper investigation of our cases there were only two sources: desk research based on materials supplied by the native lawyers; and investigation by journalists sent overseas. Without Robin Jones, the *Birmingham Evening Mail* journalist, and the information he gathered on his funded trip to Bangkok with the Smiths, I doubt I would ever have learned the truth about Karyn's story or run her campaign effectively. Most of the major cases I have written about here originated that way.

Portugal: Michael Cook

Sometimes, as a result of journalistic investigation, a case that looked straightforward and worthy of support would turn sour. One of the first cases that came to me after the launching of Fair Trials Abroad was in Portugal. In 1990, a nine-year-old British girl, Rachel Charles, had been abducted, raped and strangled. A British expat called Michael Cook, then aged thirty-eight, was arrested, 'confessed', was tried, convicted of murder and sent to prison for nineteen years.

Michael Cook had been beaten up so badly whilst in police custody that even the local honorary Consul noticed it. An *Observer* reporter investigating the case was surprised that the beating had not been reported to London. The Consular representative's explanation was a classic one. 'Are you mad? I have to live here.' The police investigation included an identity parade, which had begun and ended with a detective pointing at Mick and saying, 'Is this him?'

Nearly three years after the murder I managed to persuade Nick Davies, the investigative reporter who had written such great articles on Karyn, to go to Portugal and investigate. He wrote a major article that appeared in *The Guardian* in August 1993. There was clear evidence that the girl's stepfather, Ray Charles, had committed the murder for ransom money. Ray confessed in a local bar to drinking companion Mike Cunningham: 'Her time was up. Her time was up. She had to go and I put her down.' Three days later, Ray was confronted by another local, Bill Taylor, and eventually confessed to him. Mike Cunningham, Bill Taylor and others went to the police to tell them about Ray but the police seemed indifferent. When the trial finally opened, in February 1992, it was a disaster for Cook. As Nick Davies reported: *There were just about no hard facts in the prosecution case and so there was nothing to fight against: if the defence succeeded in producing a hard fact to help Mick Cook, the prosecution simply absorbed it and changed their case.* The judges always agreed with the prosecution. In November 1992, Ray died of cancer.

But when Nick Davies went digging he uncovered a very different story. Ray Charles may well have set up the kidnap for ransom money and killed the child, but he did not abduct her himself. The last sighting by someone who knew Rachel was at 4.25pm and a little girl, unidentified, was seen getting into the red car at 4.30pm. At that time Ray Charles had a solid alibi.

The problem was that there was also clear evidence that Mick Cook had in fact abducted the child. A teacher from Rachel's school, Kim Dring, saw him when she left her school just as Rachel was going off around the corner. He was sitting in his car near the bus stop and as she parked behind him, just before 4.30pm, he pulled away and waved at her as he went. Kim waved back as he drove around the corner because she knew him well. As Nick Davies put it: *Taking Rachel was the best fiddle yet, hardly even a crime if he was taking her with her dad's say-so, no chance of her getting hurt, and he'd get his cut of £300,000 (the ransom demand) for a day's work.* Mick Cook's family pressed him to explain what he was really doing on that Monday afternoon. On the phone to his parents in Southend, he said he could not remember. Mick Cook was released in 2002 after serving ten years in Portuguese prisons. It was the last Portuguese case of an abducted British child before Madeleine McCann.

It would be wrong to assume that the media were always on our side. Whilst we could count on the general impartiality of the broadsheets, television and radio to give our cases a fair hearing, the tabloids were a constant source of concern. I learned hard lessons about biased reporting in the immediate aftermath of Karyn's release. It was reported to me that Kelvin MacKenzie, then editor of

The Sun, approached the Smiths and offered to fly them out to Bangkok to pick up their daughter in return for an exclusive story. The Smiths, out of their sense of obligation to Robin Jones and the *Birmingham Post*, turned the offer down. 'Right,' said the editor of *The Sun*. 'We'll trash her then.' As a result Karyn faced a much divided tabloid press when she arrived home. *The Sun* and the *News of the World* went to town with every scrap of adverse information their reporters could dig up. The *Daily Mirror* and its Sunday sister paper *The People* lined up on Karyn's side simply because of the intense rivalry at the time between the two major daily and Sunday tabloids. I could always rely on the *Daily Mirror* to be on our side if *The Sun* was against us.

Britain's laws on contempt of court generally prevented the tabloids from biasing public opinion before the trial of native defendants. There was no such obstacle in the way of the tabloids when it came to Britons abroad. From the Manchester United six to Garry Mann, *The Sun* assumed that any Briton arrested on a charge of football hooliganism was guilty and ran campaigns accordingly.

Italy: Ruth Sandberg

It must have been an idyllic scene. A family gathering consisting of Ruth Sandberg and her two children – Davide, seven, and little Alexandra aged four – were having breakfast in a Venetian hotel together with the children's Italian grandparents. It was the last morning of Ruth's vacation. The family had moved the previous night from a holiday villa in northern Italy to be near Treviso airport for departure. Ruth and the children were going home to their council house in Colchester.

Suddenly, ten policemen armed with machine guns burst into the breakfast room and arrested a bewildered and shocked Ruth in front of her own children.

It took several weeks for her family, led by her brother Nick, to uncover the facts behind Ruth's predicament. The incident also came as a complete surprise to the Foreign Office. Under international law, there was no obligation to inform diplomats unless and until an arrest had taken place. What was eventually discovered was that, unknown to her, she'd been arrested for smuggling 150 kilos of cocaine into Italy and already tried and sentenced to eleven years in prison.

It wasn't until three months after her arrest that Ruth's brother Nick found his way to me. He was very suspicious since the Foreign Office had given the standard advice for families: keep away from press publicity, it can only make matters worse. However, as so many before him had found, nothing was being done to help his sister get out of jail, despite the travesty of justice behind her arrest. By this time Ruth had been transferred from a local prison in Venice to a high security prison near Milan. Her legal aid lawyer had yet to visit the court records to examine the dossier and notes of her trial.

It was now September 1998, and the Fair Trials European advisory panel of distinguished foreign lawyers had been in existence for several years. I managed to persuade Paolo Iorio, our Italian correspondent, to take up the case even though his office was in Rome. With his help, the family and I pieced together the tangled tale behind the conviction and arrest.

Ruth had led a troubled and disturbed life. She'd been adopted by a prosperous, middle-class family but ran away from home in 1978. By 1987 she had ended up in Naples and entered into a long-term relationship with a much older man. The man was Ciro di Martino, a 'building contractor', which in Naples meant much the same thing as being a 'businessman' in Moscow. He was Mafia. She travelled backwards and forwards from her home in Colchester to his home in Naples. Two years later, in 1989, on returning to Milan from Colchester she was arrested along with Martino and his friends because a quantity of cocaine had been found hidden in Martino's flat. After forty-eight hours, she was released. And that was the last time she had any personal part in the legal process until the police hauled her away from the Venice hotel to serve her sentence.

Martino remained in prison until August 1990 when he was

bailed. In 1993, after suffering constant physical abuse, Ruth left Italy to live permanently – or so she thought – in Colchester.

International law at the time allowed trials to continue in the absence of a defendant who had fled abroad at any stage of the legal process to escape justice. Of course conviction invariably followed such a trial since no defence representative was allowed to probe the case: a prosecutor's dream. This was particularly so in Italy where appropriate laws had been framed to prosecute Mafia members who usually fled abroad or went into hiding. It allowed Italian police to take a lazy way out of finding a missing defendant. All they had to do was nail the warrant of arrest, in Italian, to the door of the town hall in the municipality where the defendant had their last known address. That is what happened in Ruth's case.

Whilst on bail, Martino died of a brain haemorrhage. In March 1997 the smuggling trial opened in Naples, with the oblivious Ruth as one of nine co-accused. Ruth's absence was a godsend to the other defendants, who had clubbed together to depict Ruth as the leader of the conspiracy and a Capo de Mafia. As a result, they all got light sentences at Ruth's expense.

One would now expect to be able to get a retrial, but as Paolo Iorio, Ruth's new Italian lawyer, reported, this easy way out appeared to be blocked under Italian law. Ten years earlier another Briton was acquitted and released on a drugs charge by an Italian court. The Italian prosecution service lodged an appeal, and he was given a seven-year sentence in his absence and without his knowledge. In 1995 he returned to Italy with his family, was arrested and despite appeals all the way to the Italian Supreme Court, forced to serve his sentence.

On my advice, in Ruth's case, we immediately went to the press and a campaign was initiated by *The Observer* to bring her plight before the public. It was, after all, a sensational case involving an innocent young mother with young children. It was not only taken up by press and television generally in the United Kingdom but the Italian media joined the campaign: virtually the only case I ever had where there was favourable publicity in both countries involved. The result was an expedited bail hearing that occurred within weeks of the media reports and Ruth was released to go home, whilst the ponderous Italian justice system was left to carry on with a retrial.

Belgium: Bridget Seisay

Not all campaigns were so successful. Sometimes our clients were failed through lack of media interest. On December 23rd, 1998, only a month after the successful outcome to Ruth's case, I was winding down for Christmas. We have a family ritual in which the Christmas tree is decorated by my wife and daughter on December 22nd and it dominates the corner of the drawing room. I was sitting in my rocking chair reading a novel when the phone rang in my study next door. It turned out to be a desperate father. The voice of a very young child, constantly crying in the background and demanding attention, frequently interrupted the conversation. We hadn't got very far into his story when I realised I had a major case on my hands. If we were going to be able to do anything about it we had to move fast, before the media and the Foreign Office closed down for the holidays. I persuaded the young father to come straight over to my home, bringing his two-year-old son, as he had no one to look after the child. Perhaps we could construct a coherent story together. He arrived before lunch, but his son was distraught and such a handful that we couldn't really get going until Sally took him off to the kitchen and produced crayons, paper and whatever else we had around to distract him.

The story the father had to tell was really without parallel. His partner Bridget, mother of the child, had left home on a Saturday in November to do some Christmas shopping in Dusseldorf at one of the famous German Christmas fairs. She knew he would have no difficulty in looking after their son for forty-eight hours, and she needed the break. She went to stay with her influential cousin, an ambassador to Germany. During a drinks party at the embassy the night before her return home, the ambassador introduced her to a young woman who was also travelling to London the following day. However, she had train tickets and Bridget was due to fly. With characteristic generosity, the ambassador bought Bridget a train ticket so that the two women could travel together.

The next day was uneventful until they reached the Eurostar passport control in Brussels. The woman was detained but Bridget was allowed to go through. It turned out that the woman had been travelling on a false passport, and she immediately applied for political asylum.

Just as Bridget was about to board the train she was arrested for human trafficking. It is difficult to understand how things got that far on the evidence before the customs authorities. A few enquiries in London and Dusseldorf should have sent Bridget on her way.

The ambassador was in a quandary. He couldn't very well appear in a foreign court, so he immediately sent an official letter in support of Bridget to the authorities in Belgium. The Belgian authorities ignored the letter. By the time Bridget's partner, driven by desperation, appeared on my doorstep, a Belgian magistrate had decided there was a case to answer and she'd been sent for trial.

So how does someone, even in Flemish Belgium, get sent for trial with no tangible evidence whatsoever against them? Bridget, her partner, the ambassador and the asylum seeker were all black and of West African origin. The ambassador, being Sierra Leone's ambassador to Germany, had his evidence dismissed by the Belgian magistrate with the remark. 'We know what West African diplomats are like.' Indeed, the ambassador's letter was used by the prosecutor and accepted by the magistrates as evidence Bridget was a prostitute or a pimp engaged in trafficking the other woman. The alleged victim had already made a statement that she was travelling on her own and Bridget had nothing to do with her journey. Evidence from Bridget's employers, Tesco, stating that she was a senior cashier and her partner's evidence that they were both earning good money was also dismissed: blacks had to be poor.

It was early afternoon before I managed to take down the full story. It was time for me to get the national press and the Foreign

Office to move. In a hard-hitting article six months later, Roy Greenslade, then *The Guardian's* media editor, wrote:

It was the perfect Christmas story: a small child crying for his mother held on a preposterous charge in a foreign land. Surely the newspapers would ride to her rescue?

I contacted the obvious journalist for an emergency like this: Jo Butler, the home correspondent of the Press Association. She wrote a lengthy press release. No national newspaper took up the story. The only media team to contact me was our regional television crew, Newsroom South East. They made it their lead item on Christmas Eve, interviewing me against the background of the Christmas tree.

Meanwhile, I tried to get in touch with someone from the Consular division. I managed to raise the duty Consular department officer but he advised me that since everybody was on leave in both London and Belgium I was unlikely to get any action until the second week in January.

I spent January trying to find a good lawyer to represent Bridget in court. I eventually found Ronny Baudin, who became one of our most trusted Belgian lawyers. Using a trip subsidised by the European Parliament, I met him in Brussels to go through the court dossier. It contained no evidence at all, just a lot of magistrate's impressions.

The next three months were disastrous for Bridget. Her partner, unable to cope with the stress of Bridget's absence, lost his job. The child was referred for specialist assessment after exhibiting signs of extreme distress at his nursery school. As for myself, I had never experienced such a frustrating case. Despite my best efforts and those of Jo Butler, no national newspaper would carry the story. There was one exception; Frances Gibb of *The Times* printed one of my regular articles in the legal section in early April, just before the trial. At the trial Bridget was found guilty and sentenced to three years. It was only then that the British media woke up, and the British ambassador to Brussels announced he was pressing for a speedy appeal hearing.

Some time was spent waiting for the written version of the

magistrates' judgment. When I'd finished translating it, I realised it was one of the most racist documents masquerading as a Western Europe court decision since the fall of Nazi Germany. I sent a copy to the Foreign Office and moves must have been made behind the scenes. At any rate the appeal, when it came in June, went extremely well with the presiding judge castigating the lower court for their handling of the evidence and in particular making no moves to check out Bridget's story. A disgraceful episode had ended.

Ruth's case was one of the best and quickest results we obtained through media pressure, whilst Bridget's case was one of the worst through lack of it. So why did the press let Bridget and her family down? The two cases had much in common. Roy Greenslade and I have a theory that there is a form of 'commercial racism' in the British press. Mainstream newspapers leave cases about black people alone, because they believe that, as a minority interest, they don't sell.

17

A 'Diplomacy by Other Means' Foreign Office

Scattered through my home are a number of mementos from my legal career. In the study there is the sort of things you would expect to find: the framed certificate of enrolment as a solicitor, signed by Lord Denning, Master of the Rolls, and the certificate presented on retirement as a member of the Law Society Council. In the rest of the house there are references to my years with Fair Trials Abroad, such as the framed copy of the front page of the *Daily Telegraph* for the day Karyn came home and the GITMO (US Naval station, Guantanamo Bay) Bar Association baseball cap. But the item recalling one of the most extraordinary events I have ever attended is a simple black T-shirt, bearing the message: 'Free Ian Stillman. Deaf, disabled and a victim of injustice.'

I wore it in a cordoned-off section of pavement outside the Indian High Commission at the Aldwych. All the accompaniments of a disciplined demonstration were there: the placards, the T-shirts and the obvious commitment of the demonstrators but it was silent. Everything was being conducted in sign language. It was a 'sign in', a demonstration by deaf organisations in support of Ian. Myself and members of the Stillman family were the only hearing participants in the demo.

India: Ian Stillman

Ian Stillman's case represented one of the worst abuses of the legal process I have ever encountered. Ian became profoundly deaf at the age of two. He grew up to be one of those extraordinary characters who do not allow physical handicap to dictate their lives. While developing his mission in India he travelled everywhere by motor-bike but in 1995 he was involved in a road accident and suffered horrendous injuries, which resulted in the amputation of one of his legs above the knee. Nevertheless, with the aid of his deeply religious family and his wife, Sue, he continued to run Nambikkai, a charitable trust he founded to provide vocational training for deaf adults.

The trust grew to achieve world fame. Ian himself was the subject of a BBC documentary and by the year 2000 he had become an adviser to the Indian government on problems of deafness.

In August, that same year, he travelled to the state of Himachal Pradesh in northern India to explore the prospects of establishing a branch of the foundation there. In retrospect, it was a poor choice. Himachal Pradesh, at that time one of the poorest states in India, existed on a poisonous mixture of drug cultivation, smuggling and tourism. A number of foreign citizens had disappeared in the bandit country north of Simla and the local police were under pressure from the international community to do something about it. A visit from the British Foreign Secretary, Jack Straw, was imminent. The state police – purely for public relations purposes – needed to come up with a foreign drug smuggler, and preferably a British one, and Ian provided them with the perfect opportunity. He was clearly a handy scapegoat. It was no coincidence that he was paraded on international television within twenty-four hours of his arrest on drug smuggling charges, the day before Straw's visit.

Ian had been on his way back to his local hotel, when his taxi was stopped by a manned roadblock. The police produced a mysterious green bag containing twenty kilos of cannabis, which they later insisted in court that Ian had been clutching on his lap.

The whole case against him was a physical absurdity. Because of his artificial leg he had no 'lap' to place the bag on. Again because of the leg, he was physically incapable of carrying a weight of twenty kilos. And how does a deaf smuggler communicate? Does he get others to telephone for him on the progress of his illegal activities? No one was arrested or accused of being his accomplice.

To arrest a deaf person and pretend he can hear when you first interrogate him is bad enough, but to compound the error by maintaining this fiction throughout a long court process is a supreme injustice. Ian was convicted and sentenced to ten years, spending over two years of this in the overcrowded and unsanitary conditions of a Simla jail.

Initially, Ian and his family had decided to keep quiet for the sake of the Foundation, believing that justice would prevail and he would be released. This meant that the public campaign to free him only commenced after the appeal had failed. It took an enormous public outcry to persuade the then Foreign Secretary, Jack Straw, to act on his behalf and it would be Christmas 2002 before he received a pardon on health grounds, and was finally released.

In June 2002, I wrote an article for *The Times,* which brought to the public's attention just how badly the Foreign Office was handling such clear cases of miscarriages of justice to British citizens abroad. A fair proportion of overseas miscarriages of justice are due to human errors by law enforcers. 'Silly arrests' in mature justice systems are usually corrected very swiftly. They are not allowed to fester, so that over time the original mistake grows into a conspiracy to conceal the truth at the expense of the accused. 'Cock ups and cover-ups' are not confined to law enforcement. In my article I accused the Foreign Office of internal 'cock ups' that had reached the conspiracy stage. I also examined another case, the longest-running on our books and one of my failures.

Thailand: Alan Davies

Alan Davies had been arrested in Thailand during the Christmas of 1989 and accused, with others, of trying to sell a large quantity of heroin to a police informant. The key evidence against him, apart from the police testimony, consisted of a bank's security video, recording what had taken place. During the trial, the judges in the case issued a summons to the police to bring the video to court. The police refused to accept service of that summons. When Alan's lawyer applied to the court to enforce its own order for production, the court refused. The Chief Justice of Thailand was called in and agreed with the judges. A military government, of which the police were a part, was in power. The judiciary had no authority over the police. The court then continued to hear the case and Alan was duly convicted!

In 1994 Alan, having lost all his appeals, asked me for help. I replied saying that Karyn's case had left me with a poor reputation in Thai official circles and the wisest course for him now would be to plead guilty and agree to a prison transfer. He insisted that he would never accept guilt and instructed me to take the case.

We concentrated on the missing videos in our representations to the Foreign Office. The inter-government correspondence was slow and spasmodic. Over the next five years, various explanations were given for non-production of the videos by the Thai government: they had been lost, never existed or had been destroyed. In 1999, under renewed political pressure, the Attorney General of Thailand reviewed the case and reported that despite the absence of the videos, he was satisfied that no miscarriage of justice had taken place. This argument also satisfied the Foreign Office, until I pointed out the 'hole in my bucket' nature of the Attorney General's opinion, i.e. it was like trying to pick up water with a hole in the bucket. The Thais were missing vital evidence, the strength of which they could not gauge, and therefore the argument, like the bucket, couldn't hold water.

Eventually in May 2001, Robin Cook, the then Foreign Secretary, sent a letter of support for a full Royal pardon to his counterpart at the Thai foreign office. Unfortunately, in March 2001, two months before Cook's letter, a new official channel had been opened for a reduction of sentence which had gone unnoticed by our local Consul. The pardon support had been sent to the wrong people and joined the wrong queue. This resulted in an announcement in

October 2001 that, instead of release, Davies's life sentence would be cut to twenty-five years, leaving him with another thirteen years to serve in Thai jails. As *The Times* article stated several months later, whilst this was a terrible mistake, no attempt had been made to correct it.

Parliamentarians and lawyers were constantly misled by the Foreign Office. Assertions were made in correspondence that everything had been in order and that follow-up meetings which had never occurred had taken place in Thailand. Only one shot was allowed for a pardon, so they could do no more. The lies and excuses were endless.

We were eventually informed that the British Embassy only discovered the mistake at the end of March 2002. Meanwhile the Foreign Office had made strenuous efforts to bully Davies into accepting a prison transfer that might have resulted in a speedy release. For this to happen he would have to agree that he was guilty. He would then be left on parole in Britain for a conviction the British government agreed was wrongful. This was the reason he instructed me in the first place. I believe that it was Alan's consuming sense of injustice that kept him alive and sane during the long years of his imprisonment. He was eventually released in 2007 after serving seventeen years in a Thai jail.

Alan came to see me at my home in November 2012. Now well over seventy, he looked still older. He told me that in his early days of imprisonment, one of the things that kept him sane was learning to speak, read and write in Thai. It took him years, but he managed to teach himself with the aid of textbooks smuggled into the prison. He was mocked by a lot of the other foreign prisoners who didn't want to learn. Later on, he became a very useful friend to have, able to help them with letters, petitions and the other things they needed such as translating court documents. He could also write their appeals for them.

He became something of a prison lawyer, because it was the only way the men could help themselves. The Thai lawyers presented to them were a useless lot. Even the Thai officials – in particular the guards – used him as an interpreter, because of his usefulness with languages.

Alan described to me the time when officials came and offered him the 'blue shirt', a sort of trusty symbol that came with special status and privileges.

'I told them when you're in here, it's a case of us prisoners together and you are them [sic] and I'm not going to join you. So they offered it to a French prisoner, who took the job because of the privileges. Being a "blue shirt" meant years off the time you served, since whenever there was an amnesty with a general reduction the trusties got an extra year. For example, if there was a general five-year reduction they got six. The man who took the job eventually died of cancer. I heard after I left, that nobody, including the religious adviser, would have anything to do with him because he had changed sides.'

Alan went on:

'I could read the Thai newspapers and keep track, not only of my own case when it cropped up – which it didn't do much – but also other cases like the two girls. I heard that British Customs and Interpol wanted them to leave Thailand so that they and the gang responsible, which included a West African man who lived in Bishops Avenue, Hampstead, could be quietly arrested in the UK – but the Thais double-crossed them for the reward money.'

He revealed just how difficult it had been for him to get in touch with me. The Foreign Office had denied I existed, and despite the presence of a complete collection of British telephone directories in the Consulate, a member of the staff refused to look me up on the grounds that they had better things to do than find telephone numbers for prisoners.

I then asked him how he felt about the contact he had received from outside the prison.

'One of the things that played a big part in keeping me going was hatred of the British Foreign Office, whom I believed to be a set of duplicitous corrupt bastards from beginning to end. There were a few exceptions, all female.'

He stressed his gratitude, ending with an emphatic: 'But I really don't think very much of the rest.'

Alan continued: 'I was never actually brutally treated but I saw a lot of brutal treatment, including someone who was stamped to death in my cell. I had a mild stroke (in May 1997) and if it wasn't for a Thai doctor (in the prison for killing his wife) I would not have recovered as well as I did. The British Embassy was not good about this. Three months later a Consular representative turned up. In the presence of the other Brits she said she'd heard I had been quite poorly with some sort of heart problem – did I need a doctor? "No," said one of the others. "He needs a **** dentist!"

'We got all sorts in the prison. A conversation with a police chief who had been arrested for drug dealing was very illuminating. He was in the next cell to me and he said, "Alan, I know you're innocent, I've read the papers."

'Oh,' I replied. 'And how do you know that?'

' "Just one thing. We have a routine. We search all the premises associated with anybody who's been arrested in connection to drugs and in your case it was glaring they didn't search anywhere. They knew there were no drugs to look for and didn't want to waste their time." '

I asked Alan what the worst thing was about being in the prison.

'Being cut off from proper communication. I was also lucky that I had been taught how to cook when I was very young. Thai prison fare was totally primitive and you couldn't possibly exist off it without a supplement. One way or another, when provisions arrived, they were going to be raw.'

I wanted to know how he felt when he returned home.

'I couldn't have taken up any sort of life if it had not been for the help of Peter Brown. I got to know him because he was a pen friend of mine in prison, but I'd never met him before. He invited me to stay with him until I could get sorted out, which took me several months. I was lucky enough to sell my story to *The People* so I could survive until I went to Blackpool and managed to get my pension sorted out. Luckily I had my daughter in France to see and she sent me airline tickets and things like that. I also have my son who lives in the West Country. I am close to my late wife's extended family. She was Chinese Thai and died while I was in prison. This international network supports me wherever I go and it's been a great help to me in adjusting.'

When I first needed contact with the Foreign Office due to my representation of Karyn Smith, its scope was limited in the main to two people: Ron Dodo, the desk man for Thailand, and Christopher Denne CMG, Head of Consular Services. They were both as courteous and helpful as they could be.

In 1990, the Consular service represented the Cinderella department of the Foreign Office. Christopher Denne was a distinguished diplomat, in one of his last postings before retirement. However, as far as I could gather, he was the only 'fast track' member of the Consular services hierarchy. In general, the status of Head of Consular Services could be gauged by his or her next posting. The job was considered inferior to that of an ambassadorial role in insignificant countries.

In the beginning we exchanged information on Karyn's case and other cases both before and after the formation of Fair Trials.

The 1991 meeting on the eve of the European Parliament's decision on Karyn's case should have warned us of the shape of things to come. It was attended not only by Christopher but also by the head of the South East Asian department. This man demanded that the campaign be stopped, since it was in danger of damaging the Anglo-Thai relationship. After the meeting, Christopher told me that theoretically the two men were equal in the hierarchy of the Foreign Office.

At the heart of the problem was the dual nature of the Foreign Office. The political mainstream, the mandarins and ambassadors, is, like the Treasury, a part of internal government. The Consular section is a social service. These two functions of the FCO are often incompatible as 'the national interest' always outweighs an individual

Briton's protection overseas. Any other government, however enlightened, that combines these two functions faces the same problem.

Diplomats work on a perfectly sensible rule that bad publicity for a foreign power's justice system makes diplomatic relations very difficult: it may have an adverse affect on trade relations. In the 1970s a documentary criticising Saudi justice, *The Death of a Princess*, caused a sharp deterioration in trade relations between oil-rich Saudi Arabia and the United Kingdom, so the standard advice from Consular sources to prisoners and their families, even in extreme situations, was not to go to the press.

This made for the fundamental clash between my professional ethics working for my client and the interests of a Department of State. A lawyer is only his client's agent and must do what he is told, whether or not he agrees with it. At a meeting held in 1998 with Baroness Scotland about the Alan Davies case, I was accused of 'bloody mindedness' in taking particular courses of action. I replied that the client was entitled to be bloody-minded in view of the treatment he had received over the previous eight years by both the British and Thai authorities. The deeper problem, as was so clearly demonstrated in the *Face the Facts* programme on lorry drivers, was the culture at the time in the Foreign Office: one of patrician contempt for victims of injustice.

Early in 1994, a fellow solicitor and old friend, Andrew Phillips (Lord Phillips of Sudbury) suggested to me that I should apply for charitable status. There was an initial problem. In 1982 the Law Lords had decided that Amnesty International could not be a charitable trust, since attempting to secure the release of prisoners of conscience and procuring the abolition of torture were deemed to be political activities. We spent over a year persuading the Charity Commission secretary that seeking to apply international law on fair trial, which other countries had incorporated by treaty, was not the same thing as requiring a change in their laws.

However, things did not progress. Late in 1996, Andrew's firm,

Bates Wells Braithwaite, forced disclosure of secret correspondence about me between the then Head of Consular Division and the Secretary to the Charities Commission, a fellow civil servant. I tried to take this up with the FCO but they would not listen.

When Robin Cook became Foreign Secretary in 1997, Ann Clwyd MP, Chair of the All Party Committee on Human Rights, contacted him, showing concern about this letter. The reply just repeated the false allegations.

We held a crisis trustees meeting and agreed the draft of a letter to Robin Cook. Our letter ran to three pages. It protested that a bizarrely inaccurate portrayal of my part in Karyn's case had been given in the secret letter, including the allegation that I made attacks on Her Majesty's Customs and Excise, attributing Nick Davies's article on their activities to me. They made no distinction between our commission from the European Union to compile a database of EU lawyers, speaking English, French, German and Spanish for the use of all EU citizens, and a British Consular list of English-speaking lawyers for the use of British citizens. The FO had also told the Charity Commission that we charged for our services.

In December, a reply came from Robin Cook, drafted by civil servants running for cover. That letter also ran to three pages. The general line taken was that the poor civil service had been confused on various counts, and in particular, bewildered by changes in the title of the organisation before it became a Trust. The Trust had already been in existence for over three years at the time of the original letter to the Charities Commission. The letter started: '*I regret that we are having to enter into this correspondence,*' and ended '*I hope that this letter will conclude this correspondence... I understand the Baroness Symons has agreed to meet you... I welcome this opportunity for you to raise your concerns with her and to tell her more about the work of your organisation.*' It was the nearest thing we would get to an apology. We left it at that.

Although there were variations in the relationship for the next two years, it was greatly improved.

The change should be attributed to two strong Ministers of State, Baronesses Symons and Scotland, who took no nonsense from their advisers, even though we often disagreed. There was also a revolution occurring in the quality of their staff. The practice had begun of shifting high fliers around, moving them every two years through all the departments of the Foreign Office, including the Consular Division. The bad news was the loss of long-term experienced executives to retirement, and the substitution of bright youngsters who had just about mastered their job before moving on.

Then in February 2000 I received a telephone call from a new number two in the Consular Division, inviting me to have lunch with him and discuss matters of mutual interest. I knew of Matthew Gould. In his first assignment overseas as a lowly second secretary in the Philippines Embassy, the undiplomatic strength and forcefulness in championing our client Albert Wilson had been noteworthy. Wilson, who had been imprisoned since 1992 and convicted on a fabricated charge of rape of his stepdaughter, won his appeal in 1999 and came home.

At our meeting, Matthew told me he was keen to do what he could to help victims of injustice and asked me to act as his adviser on policy and procedure. It was revolutionary talk from a young diplomat still only in his twenties. Later that day I wrote a letter that dealt with the discussed topics: lists of lawyers, the application of international rules on fair trial and the importance of early intervention in clear cases. It was the beginning of our close cooperation.

In April 2000, when we finally achieved charitable status, we threw a party to celebrate. We invited the families of clients old and new to join us. Matthew, on hearing about this, wanted to join us to get to know the clients. He was the most senior Foreign Office official ever to attend one of our functions during my watch.

Perhaps the most important thing we accomplished was the brief we put together on the need to change the grounds for supporting pardons. Before then, the only grounds for a pardon had been prisoner's health or family emergencies. We wanted to include miscarriages of justice. We succeeded in obtaining the change of policy in 2001 and the first beneficiary of that change was Alan John Davies.

In December 2001 Matthew was posted at short notice. Within

forty-eight hours of Matthew's leaving, his boss – the Head of Consular Division – pretended that the changes we made had never happened. I had been invited to the Foreign Office Christmas party and ran into Matthew there. He told me that his boss's pretence that our agreements and policy changes were unknown to the department was an exercise in 'deniability'. They had definitely been circulated and agreed within the department.

One of the ideas we put forward was to draw up a list of reliable British volunteers, who could be trained by our team to assist in overseas cases generally. We could only handle a small number of cases by ourselves. As soon as Matthew had gone, the FCO set up its own advisory panel by personal invitation. The volunteers would vet any applications for Consular support and become a sole pool of advisers for Consular referrals.

I learned about the new list by accident. I enquired why Sabine and I – the only two people who had extensive experience of Britons facing criminal trial overseas – hadn't been asked. We were told we didn't qualify. A copy of the FCO list revealed it was mainly composed of entire firms of solicitors, including trainees. I asked again and was told it was because of our attitude to publicity.

This particular Head of Consular Division personally visited Ian Stillman's family in a failed attempt to persuade them to drop us and use one of his panel. His real attitude towards Ian's plight was his message of complaint to me that, as a result of the article in *The Times*, he had received so many letters in support of Ian that he'd been forced to detail two of his staff full-time to reply to them!

The Trust was extremely concerned by these tactics. I complained to the president of the Law Society about the clear interference in solicitor/client relationships involved. It was the FCO, not the client, who decided not only who was on the list but which solicitor would be put forward to represent the individual client. Those who did not follow the FCO line would lose out.

We need not have worried. The result was risible. A steady stream of young or inexperienced members of the panel appeared in our offices, begging for help with their assigned cases.

It was inevitable that things had to change. The Foreign Office had badly misjudged their credibility with the British public and the Blair administration was nothing if not PR-conscious. Baroness Symons came back to take charge of Consular affairs and there was a rapid turnaround in the Foreign Office relationship due to a warm rapport with Jack Straw, the new Secretary of State.

By 2003 we were holding regular case meetings with the Consular Department. Much to my surprise, I was given an OBE in the New Year's honours of 2005 – on the Foreign Office list!

And that is what I thought had happened until I recently came across *The New Mandarins,* an authorised account of the workings of the Foreign Office written as long ago as 2004 by the then Daily Mirror diplomatic correspondent John Dickie. In his preface, Dickie states that he realised that his treatise depended on assessing how a quiet revolution begun by Young Turks in the Foreign Office changed the system and made it more open to ideas from both them and outside influence. It could only have worked with encouragement and support by two successive permanent undersecretaries, Sir John Kerr and Sir Michael Jay (now Lord Jay and a patron). Discussing the limits of NGO influence, Dickie stated:

This drove home the limitations of NGO influence. Whilst there are often occasions when the objectives of government coincide with those of NGOs, making cooperation with them advantageous, there are times when the conscience of the NGOs finds no response in the harsh realities of the world in which government has to operate.'

As he then observed:

... cooperation created a relationship unimagined in the 1990s when an 'us' and 'them' attitude prevailed in most contacts between the Foreign Office and the NGOs. It is welcomed by the smaller NGOs, who have no reservations about working with the government when this increases the prospect of achieving their objectives. NGOs are prepared to put at the disposal of government the sort of information that official diplomatic resources are in no position to obtain without undermining their status in the country.

The leader of the Young Turks was Matthew Gould.

Part 5: Campaigns

18

Guantánamo

The aftermath of the atrocity that occurred on September 11th, 2001, and the struggle to get European citizens out of concentration camps set up by the United States was to dominate the last years of my work. I was involved from the start, but it was the plight of Moazzam Begg and his family that reinforced the lesson that the disgrace of institutionalised injustice is a sum total of individual tragedies.

When the first plane struck, Sally was up a ladder in our daughter's new flat painting the ceiling. The radio was on and she believed the newsflash to be part of a play. With the chilling announcement of the second plane hitting, she said she knew the World had changed and nothing would be the same again. She was right. At the time, I was so engrossed with cross-border arrangements for criminal justice that the bigger picture succeeded in passing me by.

The morning of September 11th, 2001, I attended a meeting with a conservative MEP at the European Parliament building in Brussels. We were busy discussing his imminent tour of India when an aide rushed in from the adjoining room and said we must see what was happening in New York. We switched on CNN and saw a replay of the first attack on the Twin Towers. The view changed and to our horror we witnessed a second attack happening, live! We were still absorbing what we had just seen when the public address ordered us to evacuate the building. We all left and congregated on the pavement in the square at the back of Parliament. The crowds we were expecting did not materialise; in fact it was only the British and Spaniards who joined us. We never quite got to the bottom of this false alarm. Evidently some form of attack or bomb scare involving ETA had been received and security had panicked. Since the alarm had been selectively angled at the Spanish, while someone else had rebroadcast it in English, they had forgotten to use the other languages of the Union and so no one else took the alert seriously.

After a while of mooching around on the pavement, some of us went for a coffee – or something stronger – in the string of restaurants, pubs and cafes lining the other side of the square. Others, including me, drifted back inside.

The September trip had been a carefully planned Brussels 'milk run' until the destruction of the Twin Towers. Sarah and I were preoccupied with the Tampere conclusions – the original communiqué at the end of the justice summit two years earlier which had succeeded in establishing the European Legal Space (a common area of justice for the European Union). There was nothing in the conclusions – and the relatively leisurely programme adopted as a result – to allay our concerns about the tipping of the scales of justice due to the vast new powers being given to prosecutors. A critical paper was at the final stages of preparation by the European Parliament and it would be placed before the Civil Liberty Committee at a meeting scheduled for September 12th. We also had a mountain of casework meetings with MEPs and a number of other meetings concerning our potential grant for the following year. The schedule had been thrown into chaos. 'Keep calm and carry on' may be a great slogan for the Northern Europeans but didn't seem to work so well with the Latin temperament.

The first meeting on September 12th was with Graham Watson; still Chair of the Civil Liberties Committee, and the secretary, Emilio de Capitani. We had a huddled emergency conference in the entrance lobby just before the committee meeting was due to begin. It was clear to us all that the first priority for the international community had to be the fight against global terrorism. Our mood was that of William Pitt on hearing the news of the Battle of Austerlitz, Napoleon's decisive land victory. When he saw the map of Europe on the wall, it called forth one of his most famous comments: 'Roll up that map, it will not be wanted these ten years'. We shared the thought that any progress on citizens' rights would not be made for a decade and we were just going through the motions. In hindsight that was about right.

The immediate consequent events – the war following the discovery that Osama bin Laden, the architect of 9/11 was being 'hosted' by Mullah Omar, leader of the Taliban and head of the Government of Afghanistan – seemed nothing to do with us.

The Bush Administration then faced the problem of what to do with non-Afghan prisoners and those they considered might have something to do with the 9/11 atrocity. Whilst potential traitors, those nationals of the UN who fought for the Taliban may have committed crimes, these were national crimes and the United States could only try US citizens on that basis.

On the face of it, international law was relatively uncomplicated. The Geneva Convention applies in wars between two or more sovereign states to all detainees. Four treaties and three additional protocols established the standards of international law. The singular term 'Geneva Convention' denotes the agreements of 1949, which updated the terms of the first three treaties (1864, 1906, 1929), and added a fourth treaty. The articles of the Fourth Geneva Convention comprehensively defined the basic rights of prisoners (civil and military) during war. It is settled law that every person in enemy hands must be either a prisoner of war and, as such, be covered by the Third Convention; or a civilian covered by the Fourth Convention. There is no intermediate status; nobody in enemy hands can be outside the law. The United States is a party to all four conventions.

The law for anyone that passed through American or Allied hands was clear enough.

1. The status of a detainee may be determined by a 'competent tribunal'. Until such time, he is to be treated as a prisoner of war.

2. If this tribunal has determined that an individual detainee is an unlawful combatant, the US government may choose to accord the detained unlawful combatant the rights and privileges of a prisoner of war but is not required to do so.

3. An unlawful combatant must be 'treated with humanity and, in case of trial, shall not be deprived of the rights of fair and regular trial'.

Whatever the United States wished to do with people it had detained as a result of the war, the international rules of fair trial had to be observed.

Until January 2002, when prisoners taken as a result of the war began to arrive at Guantánamo, not many people had heard of the obscure camp in the American base in Cuba. In the 1990s it had been used as a transit camp for Cuban refugees to Florida and known as Camp X-Ray. Camp Delta, the new specialist prisoners' holding area, was opened a couple of months later and at its height held over 600 prisoners of the Americans. Court facilities were built into the complex and it became clear that the United States Government was going to try certain prisoners under military law.

The reason why this base was used as a dumping ground for the foreign prisoners was because it was held from the Cubans under a lease, which the Bush administration hoped made it non-sovereign territory. For this reason, the US Federal justice system would be unable to adjudicate on the fairness of any trial system the Bush administration decided to use. President Bush was determined that the niceties of the law were not going to get in the way of punishing 'those folks' – as he quaintly called the perpetrators of 9/11 and all their allies – in the first shock of the atrocity.

Right at the beginning, a number of European citizens turned up amongst the prisoners, specifically British and French. The national communities of human rights lawyers – most prominent amongst them the British, centred round Gareth Peirce and Linda Christian – began to stir into action. From the outset I was determined that we would provide the European input and stand by the principles of international law. As soon as the prisoners began to arrive in Guantánamo, I announced our policy in a letter to *The Guardian.*

Letters, *The Guardian,* 18th January, 2002

Dear Sir

Fair trial for the captives

I am concerned by the confusion that could be caused by the statement in today's article that Mr Rumsfeld is not responsible for the legal process in the United States of America. Of course as a general proposition that is true but it may not be in this case.

Mr Rumsfeld is in control of the armed services. He acts in the role of prosecutor by his public statements. International law requires an unbiased and independent tribunal to preside over trials. It is impossible to understand how the type of tribunal required to match up to requirements of Justice can possibly be satisfied by appointing its members from amongst those who are under his orders. Military tribunals are out.

I do not believe that international law can deny the United States its right to try those suspected of being involved in acts of terror on its soil. However, the difficulties of conducting fair trials against a background of national outrage are not to be underestimated. Perhaps the way forward is to use the Lockerbie experience where those accused of being involved in a terrorist act that cost a large number of American and British fatalities on Scottish soil were tried by a tribunal of senior Scottish Judges. What is wrong with appointing a tribunal of federal Judges chaired by a Supreme Court Justice?

Sincerely,

Stephen Jakobi

Director

Fair Trials Abroad

This policy eventually put me on a tactical collision course with a number of prominent British human rights lawyers. I remember Linda Christian trying to persuade me, just before we went on a television news programme, that her strategy to 'Bring Them Home' i.e. to get them into the United Kingdom to be tried under British law, was the right one. For my part I stuck to our policy, the only one that seemed to work under international law with a good precedent, Lockerbie, to guide us.

Letters, *The Guardian*, 14th February, 2002

Dear Sir

Speaking for Justice

In your otherwise thoughtful leader 'Speak for Britain' you omitted to mention the looming problem of justice for those Britons and other Europeans awaiting possible trial in Camp x-ray. On page 18 (Stunt aims to turn US jury against Taliban suspect) Matthew Engel reports on the latest court appearance in the Federal legal proceedings against John Lindh 'the American Taliban'. His treatment with all the guarantees of the American constitution is in marked contrast to what may be planned for the Europeans and others.

President Bush issued an order on Nov. 13 authorizing the use of military tribunals to try non-U.S. citizens accused of terrorist acts. The American Bar Association has raised concerns that the military tribunals would jeopardize civil and due process rights of prisoners and prevent them from receiving fair trials.

Among specific concerns are that the trials could be held in secret, defendants could be barred from seeing the evidence against them, only a two-thirds vote would be needed to impose the death penalty and the standard for conviction would be lower than 'beyond a reasonable doubt'.

At our suggestion, Cecilia Malmström, a Swedish MEP, initiated an urgency resolution in the European parliament, passed last week, on the treatment of the detainees in Guantánamo Bay that included expressions of concern with regard to the judicial process they were likely to undergo. The Swedish government are expressing public concern about the position of their three citizens. May we now hear it from Tony Blair?

Sincerely,

Stephen Jakobi

Director

Fair Trials Abroad

It had been Sarah Ludford's suggestion that I approach Cecilia Malmström to pilot through an urgency resolution on the

Guantánamo situation. I pictured a fifty-something MEP. I did manage to meet her on a regular Brussels visit and was totally taken aback to find someone under thirty. I was bowled over by one of the most charismatic politicians I have ever met in Brussels. The only other young politician I met there who could stand comparison was the young Nick Clegg, who for a short time acted as our political adviser before returning to Britain.

Cecilia's subsequent career has been meteoric. She returned to Sweden to become the Cabinet Minister for European Affairs and is still in her early forties working in Brussels as Commissioner for Home Affairs. She not only shares her politics with Nick Clegg, she is also, like him, a polyglot. She is fluent in Swedish, English, Catalan, Spanish and French and she also has a good standard of German and Italian. Somehow along the way she has managed to bear and bring up twins with her husband in Brussels. We are familiar with high-powered Scandinavian women from various television series and to me she is Birgette Nyborg, the Danish Prime Minister in *Borgen* (without the dysfunctional family life).

Her European Parliament resolution on the detainees in Guantánamo Bay was nearly 600 words long but the main points were:

- *That it believed that all the detainees regardless of their nationality or origin should have the same treatment;*
- *Calls therefore on the UN and its Security Council to pass a resolution establishing a tribunal to deal with Afghanistan, with the aim of clarifying the prisoners' legal status;*
- *Believed that these difficulties would have been much easier to resolve with a fully functioning international criminal court with jurisdiction over acts of terrorism;*
- *Concluding with instructing its President to forward the resolution to the Council, the Commission, the US Government, the US Congress and the United Nations.*

Given the general confusion and lack of information we all suffered from at this stage of the Guantánamo debacle it wasn't a bad resolution as emergency resolutions go. We did much better with the considered resolution of 2004.

I was desperate to the point of foolhardiness in my efforts to wake up United States citizens to the abuse of law involved in the Bush administration's rules regarding Guantánamo. After early television debates on Sky with a number of partisan Republican lawyers who seemed totally oblivious to both the Geneva conventions and international law, I wrote to *The New York Times*, just after the European Parliament resolution.

Robert Verkaik of *The Independent* described what happened next during the course of an article celebrating the 10th anniversary of the foundation of FTA by its launch in his newspaper.

Nothing prepared the Director of the campaigning group Fair Trials Abroad for the ferocity of the abuse from New Yorkers that followed his intervention in the debate over Camp X-ray.

All he had suggested was that the detainees being held at Guantánamo Bay in Cuba deserved a fair hearing. The next day his e-mail postbag was bulging with messages from New York cabbies telling him to mind his own business – but couched in language closer to the street parlance of Robert De Niro in the film Taxi Driver.

A more cultured voice from across the sea suggested that if he was so keen to see the al-Qa'ida [sic] and Taliban suspects properly treated, why didn't he offer to put them up in his own home?

In a letter to The New York Times *he said he realised he was addressing the newspaper of choice for many of those who live in the area surrounding ground zero in Manhattan, where the personal losses were heaviest and feelings run strongest. But he said that, at a time when the world was watching planeloads of prisoners being flown into Cuba, American justice would be forever judged on the treatment of these 'helpless' detainees.*

'As I understand it,' he wrote, 'smoke signals are coming from the United States administration that a military tribunal is being contemplated. Yet already your Secretary of Defense is acting in the role of prosecutor by stating publicly that these detainees represent the hard core of the terrorist organisations. It is impossible to understand how the type of tribunal required can match up to requirements of justice when its members are being drawn from those who are

under his orders.' Since he wrote these words his flood of hate mail has dropped to a trickle.

For me, 2002 was a fire-fighting year. I was preoccupied with some major cases: I travelled to India for the Ian Stillman case, and of course to Greece for the planespotters. The other campaign for justice for Europeans in Europe seemed to be the priority. I only kept a watching brief on Guantánamo. In March 2002, Donald Rumsfeld, the American Defence Secretary, issued Military Commission Order Number One that set out procedures to be employed in the trials of the Guantánamo prisoners. There was a chorus of alarm from American and British defence lawyers in which we joined. Our press release honed in on the basics:

Parity of arms is the essence of fair trial and this means that both prosecution and defence have equal access to all available evidence. Limiting disclosure to the defence in any way of evidence fully available to the prosecution must mean a biased and unfair trial. Other concerns relate to the independence of the Tribunal. We await full details and urge that more thought is given to the rules.

Apart from that it wasn't until the early summer of 2003 that the emotional telephone call from Azmet Begg threw me back into hectic activity on the Guantánamo issue.

At this time all our hopes were centred on a projected visit by Tony Blair to Washington to receive a Congressional Medal of Honour and address both Houses of Congress as a reward for being the United States staunchest ally in the second Iraqi war. He had also declared that all the prisoners in Guantánamo deserved a fair trial. Surely he could get something done about the British prisoners?

Sarah Ludford, long-time patron of FTA and my closest ally in Europe, produced a motion in the European Parliament on the eve of this key meeting:

A text similar to that of the Early Day Motion in the House of Commons (which currently has 221 signatures) has already been signed by members of the European Parliament from the UK, Sweden, Denmark, Germany, Italy, Greece, Ireland, Portugal and Belgium. More signatures are expected.
She said: 'We've been told many times that Mr Blair enjoys a special

relationship with George Bush. For me and my European colleagues, this
meeting with Bush is a critical test of that.

'*With concern in the House of Commons matched by concern in the*
European Parliament, Mr Blair must decide on his priorities. Is he a "critical
friend" securing justice for UK and other EU citizens by upholding values
common to Europe and America? Or is he no more than the President's poodle,
satirised by press and politicians alike?'

It is history that the meeting was a fiasco. It was immediately
followed by what can only be called a display of public folly by the
President of the United States in a televised press conference. The
immediate aftermath was to be a visit by the British Chief Law
Officer, Lord Goldsmith, to Washington to discuss details of the
limited options available. My own press release was quoted across
the world:

The latest developments have clearly sent Lord Goldsmith off on a mission
impossible. Acting as we do as co-ordinators of the international campaign for
the rights of the EU citizens detained, we are astounded that it has been
announced by Tony Blair that the Attorney General is to discuss only two
options. The return of the British and Australian prisoners to their native
countries or making the military tribunal fair.

The original rationale was one law for US citizens and another law for the
rest of us. The bizarre outburst of prejudicial remarks by Bush at the Bush
Blair press conference on Thursday rules out fair trial by way of Military
Tribunal, whatever fig leaves can be negotiated. Having ruled out the other
options of bringing those selected for trial to ordinary US civilian justice by
transporting them to the mainland, or bringing US civilian justice to the
prisoners with a Lockerbie style system, leaves an all or nothing approach that is
in fact a desperate gamble. To send the nine Britons home and forget about the
rest would fracture the Blair doctrine of European/USA alliance since it would
leave the three Frenchmen, the Dane, the Swede and the Spaniard imprisoned in
Guantánamo remaining as lesser breeds without the law.'

One can only hope that poor old Lord Goldsmith managed to
clock up enough frequent flyer coupons on whatever airline he
employed to get a good holiday at the end of the exhausting shuttle
diplomacy that stretched out until November and beyond. I met

him, together with the other NGOs, on a number of occasions in London during the course of it.

The political season of 2002/3 came to an end within days of the Bush/Blair meeting. Azmet Begg and I conferred on how we could further the pressure in the days ahead. There was nothing we could do during August, but September gave us two possibilities. I found out he was a card-carrying member of the Liberal Democrats. There was bound to be an emergency debate on Guantánamo at the conference and I managed to get a speaking slot for both of us at the conference through negotiations with the organising committee.

The Liberal Democratic conference kicked off, as ever, the major parties' conference season. We made the front page of *The Guardian* on September 25th:

As delegates voted for Liberal Democrat MPs to unanimously oppose the treaty, the father of one of the nine Britons held at the Camp Delta detention centre in Cuba wept as he recalled how his son phoned him from the boot of a car to break the news of his capture, and how he had written saying he was being treated like an 'animal'. He pleaded for the US to allow him a British trial.

Azmet Begg, a Liberal Democrat, told delegates his son Moazzam – seized in Pakistan in February 2002 and transferred to the camp a year later – should face justice and be punished if found guilty. But he added: 'I don't understand under what law… he has been kept there. I do not say set him free. What I say is let him come back to this country.'

Mr Begg, from Sparkbrook, Birmingham, said his son phoned him when he was first arrested and said: 'Daddy, I have been arrested and kidnapped. I'm speaking from the boot of a car.'

The director of Fair Trials Abroad, Stephen Jakobi, said he was moved to 'break cover' as a Liberal Democrat and speak at the conference, because Guantánamo Bay posed the greatest challenge ever faced by his organisation.

By now I had written the third of a series of briefings for parliamentarians on Guantánamo and was the established legal adviser to the Europeans. Sarah Ludford and other parliamentarians planned a half-day conference in Brussels taking place on September 30th, less than a week after the Liberal Democrat conference. Sarah De Mas was heavily involved in the behind-the-scenes organisation. The theme was 'Guantánamo: the right to a fair trial' and one of the large meeting rooms in the European Parliament was packed. The meeting had been organised by the four parties that represented a majority in the European Parliament. It was co-chaired by Ms Anna Terron I Cusi (Socialist), Baroness Ludford (Liberal), Marianne Eriksson (Radical Left) and Ms. Monica Frassoni (Greens).

The method of proceeding was unusual. We had managed to locate a number of family representatives and their lawyers from different countries. Since some of female family representatives were very shy, each of the family rep/lawyer units were allotted ten minutes to speak, and it was up to them how their time was divided. Those present were:

- Nayat Abderahman, sister of the Spanish detainee Hamed Abderahman
- Aymen Sassi, brother of the French detainee Nizar Sassi
- Medhi Ghezali, father of the Swedish detainee Medhi Ghezali
- Azmet Begg, father of British detainee Moazzam
- Bernhard Docke, German lawyer of a Turkish detainee, to give the view of a detainee being born and having always lived in an EU country but without having European Citizenship

It was the first and only time where a multinational collection of affected Guantánamo families got together during the entire Guantánamo/European saga. It was a highly emotional and har-rowing session. The impression I gathered from hearing the families' experiences was that of a general bewilderment at the extraordinary situation they been placed in; the transition from ignorance of any involvement in Afghanistan of closest family members, to doubt and concern at their treatment in the hands of authority. Above all, they were concerned about the almost total lack of family communication. In the fifteen months or so that Azmet was aware of his son's incarceration he had only received heavily censored letters at intervals of six weeks or so. It was reminiscent of the relatives' experience of communication with inmates of Nazi prisoner-of-war camps in the Second World War, with added censorship. We could only suspect that it was to prevent details of ill-treatment reaching the outside world.

There was then an hour's break during which a German TV journalist who had just come back from Guantánamo and Afghanistan showed some of his film material. The conditions in the camps for prisoners were horrendous. The 'cells' were metal cages open to the sky yet it had recently been declared unlawful in Europe to keep chickens in such conditions. Things were due to 'improve'. The United States Military were constructing a more permanent complex complete with courtroom – and execution chamber!

At 5.30pm the general debate began. I spoke after the Parliamentary affairs officer of the US mission to the EU. Although there were a number of interruptions to his bullet-proof vest exposition of the Bush doctrine on the camps, torture, etcetera, he managed to escape unlynched. In retrospect, this was actually the seminal meeting for generating a cohesive European response.

I had to focus on the Guantánamo situation for the next six months. A number of developments occurred almost simultaneously. In November, I was invited to New York to meet up with the American defenders. The European Parliament decided to create a joint committee composed of members of the Civil Liberties in Human Rights Committees to investigate and propose a comprehensive resolution on the Guantánamo situation for a plenary session. Sarah Ludford was one of the *rapporteurs* and I was formally appointed legal adviser. A week later Bush visited London and we saw the result of Goldsmith's months of shuttle diplomacy.

I was invited to attend a weekend conference in New York of the Civil Coalition for Constitutional Rights (3CR), a standing body being set up in the United States to deal with the Guantánamo problem. In the previous eighteen months, numbers had risen from 200 to over 600. There had been a previous conference on an Anglo-British basis to see how British lawyers could help the US defence attorneys in bringing the issues of Guantánamo to the Supreme Court. It was hoped that the Supreme Court would declare the administration's actions unconstitutional. I was, I think, the only British practising lawyer present at this particular conference.

Through my jetlag, I had hazy memories of the conference room in New York Law School. There was a display of head coverings, from skullcaps of orthodox Jews to a ten-gallon hat worn by a Texan attorney. Baseball hats with the logo 'Guantánamo Bay Bar Association' and a palm tree were handed out at the end of the day. Supper and some drinking was done with Clive Stafford Smith, the eminent British human rights lawyer, and an Australian associate of his. Clive is an extraordinary mixture of manic drive and intellectual prowess, which he directs to extreme views on crime and punishment. He didn't seem to need sleep. He and his wife left us after midnight on a later occasion to fly to New York at four o'clock the same morning.

Here the idea of a Guantánamo European Support Group was informally discussed and key players identified. I returned home and circulated a plan of action to our allies in the European Parliament and Commission:

The purpose of the group is to assist the GITMO group in their endeavours to obtain due process for the inmates of Guantánamo bay by both judicial and political means. The initial aim is to concentrate on the plight of the twenty or so European citizens since this strategy is most likely to produce a positive response from European institutions both national and international.

... Fair Trials Abroad will attempt to lead and co ordinate the campaign within the EU at European, National and Professional level. It will have the advice and assistance of other European members in this task.

The Fair Trials Abroad team of Sarah, Sabine and I were all involved, Sarah maintaining close links with the European lawyers acting for the European detainees, Spanish and Dutch Governments, Sabine as caseworker and German/Austrian link. In particular, Gareth Peirce advised us as Moazzam Begg's British lawyer and was our help on Muslim sensibilities.

An immediate worry was the Military Tribunal timetable, just as the dead Christmas season was almost upon us: *Charges will be announced and proceedings commence January 2004. Defendants to be allowed only 30 days to appoint and brief Consul including Civilian Consul.*

We had worked out a preliminary support strategy for Europeans. On the judicial side we had been informed:

The court will accept Amicus Briefs from Governments, from Governmental organisations and professional groups. These must be lodged before the deadline in December and should be angled to impress upon the court that both international law and international opinion are against the Tribunal procedure.

Unfortunately, the constitutional legal advisers to the European Parliament gave advice that although Parliament was a sovereign body, it did not have the competence to file Amicus briefs and a plenary session resolution was the best we could do.

There was a problem in tackling representation. It needed to be paid for. Again, restrictions on funds available to the European Parliament left it unable to help. The most urgent task was to lobby for the EU parliament resolution to be passed in the December plenary.

We were hopeful that the Bush state visit to London, scheduled for 19–21 November, 2003, would make useful concessions on the military tribunal. In an eve-of-visit press release we pointed out: *Although the British represent the largest group (10) there are at least 6 French, a Swede, a Dane and a Spaniard amongst the detainees.*

We emphasised how little we knew at that stage about the detainees. Independent access had been confined to the Red Cross, who had publicly and unprecedentedly complained both about their difficulties in obtaining access and the mental state of detainees. We again referred to our main source as 'family information gleaned from infrequent, heavily censored and out of date letters delivered by the Red Cross'.

The visit resulted in minor cosmetic changes, such as the gracious announcement that the death penalty wouldn't be sought for British prisoners.

January 2004 saw me in Brussels to take part in the joint committee session preparing for the plenary resolution on Guantánamo. The need to provide seating in a conference room designed for a smaller EU membership left me without a seat connected to the simultaneous translation system. Since it was my role at the end of the session to answer members' queries and observations, I couldn't really sit there deaf to all those who weren't prepared to speak English or French. I explained to the Secretary of the Committee my dilemma and they found one vacant seat, scheduled for a member who hadn't turned up. About halfway through the session I noticed some peculiar looks from the press representatives. My place card bore the name of Mussolini! I understand she was a far right MEP and *Il Duce's* granddaughter.

As so often happens in crowded sessions, the ten minutes I was originally allotted to make the reply shrank in the course of the proceedings to two minutes. When I intervened to protest that I hadn't got enough time, I was told by the chairman that members had to make do so I'd better do the best I could. It was a poor best, but probably lobbying had already left things cut and dried. I told them: 'It is clear to me that we have arrived at an end game that is likely to result in the return of all the European prisoners held in Guantánamo to their native lands... we may anticipate a mixed result with, perhaps, two of the Britons and possibly other Europeans being left for trial in Guantánamo Bay.'

By February, we knew where we were. Another press statement:

We appear to have reached a staging post in the ongoing illegal detention of European citizens in Guantánamo Bay. Arrangements have now been made for a number of citizens to return home... A good time for an overview of the situation.

The nationality of those being returned should be noted. Six EU countries had citizens imprisoned. The Spaniard, Dane and some of the Britons have been released. The Swede, Belgians and French remain in Guantánamo at the time of writing this letter. It is surely no coincidence that Spain, Denmark and the UK supported the US in its Iraq venture and Sweden, Belgium and France opposed it. Clearly the United States has been linking release of prisoners to politics rather than their ostensible reason for continued detention, the 'war' against terror.

The continuing efforts to obtain the return of those EU citizens left in the legal limbo of Guantánamo also vary. One has no doubt that the governments of France, Sweden and the United Kingdom will persist in their separate bilateral negotiations to ensure that their remaining prisoners either face due process in Guantánamo or are returned home. However, the Belgian Government in a disgraceful display of impotence has publicly announced that they will abandon the two Belgians to the current unfair procedure.

The European Parliament has made its will known in its recent plenary motion calling upon the European Council to negotiate collectively, and surely at least the Belgians will recognise the folly of bilateralism.'

A couple of months later, the rest of the European citizens were released on a plea by the Irish presidency to Bush when he visited Dublin. We were quite wrong in our initial reaction to the Guantánamo situation. I think, without exception, all those outside the United States believed that Blair's close relationship with George Bush would result in a quicker solution. The British government had accomplished nothing through acting alone.

Maajid Nawaz and the Egyptian Three

The 'Egyptian Three' case, although their arrests took place in 2002, was in many respects ahead of its time. It involved the later-disgraced regime of President Mubarak, torture, disregard for legal niceties, a hatred of the Muslim Brotherhood and similar organisations. It belongs here, with Guantánamo.

Maajid Nawaz, Ian Nisbet, and Reza Pankhurst were arrested in Cairo. Nisbet and Pankhurst had travelled to Egypt to study Arabic and started a computer company in Cairo, whilst Nawaz was learning Arabic in Egypt as a part of his university course. The three men were accused of belonging to – and campaigning for – the Islamic Liberation Party, Hizb ut-Tahrir.

After their arrests they were denied access to their Consulate for eleven days. During this time they were tortured with, amongst other methods, electric shock treatment. Nevertheless, Reza Pankhurst managed to insert words such as 'lies' and 'hurt' into his signature when forced to sign confessions and other documents under extreme duress. The allegations of torture occurring during this time were never investigated.

The Egyptian Three eventually faced charges of the promotion of the goals of Hizb ut-Tahrir, using both the written and the spoken word; and the possession and distribution of printed literature, together with a printing instrument for the same. This turned out to be a computer, which was hardly surprising considering Reza Pankhurst's occupation as an IT Consultant. The fact that neither Egypt nor Britain had ever issued a legal decree banning Hizb ut-Tahrir did not seem to figure in the equation.

The trial took place at the (Emergency) Supreme State Security Court in Cairo. This bizarre court clearly violated international fair trial standards as, amongst other objectionable practices, it denied the defendants the right to appeal a verdict. At one stage, the Egyptian judiciary delayed proceedings for a full five months, with no mitigating reason. Similarly they postponed issuing the verdict for a further three months.

Throughout the entire trial, the men experienced no access to an interpreter and the judge had to order the prosecution to provide specific articles of evidence. The verdict was finally delivered in March 2004, with each man receiving a five-year sentence. That left them two years to serve, as they had already spent three in prison from the time of their arrest. Their release was due in 2006. It was almost the last case I handled before retirement.

On Tuesday, 28th February, 2006, we were told that the Egyptian three were coming home. Sabine had prepared the case and we were working closely together. We imposed a news blackout. Having issued an overnight press statement I was due, at the request of the family, to meet the three at the airport at 7am on Wednesday morning and handle the inevitable airport press conference for them. Of course, we weren't sure what shape they'd be in when they arrived.

It was about 4.30pm on Tuesday afternoon when Sabine, a regular *Times* reader, contacted me to say that *The Times* seemed to have got wind of this release and had a printed a short paragraph that morning stating that Blair was in favour of banning Hizb ut-Tahrir over here on the grounds that they were a terrorist organisation that advocated violent overthrow of our government. It was late and I was about to settle the press release. We obviously had some urgent checking to do since neither of us was willing to act for members of a violent organisation and if need be we would have to pull out rather publicly. We were relieved to find out that the Association of Chief Constables was not in favour of banning Hizb ut-Tahrir. I also contacted two of the three wives and they confirmed that Hizb ut-Tahrir was peaceable.

Although the FCO had assured us that there would be no trouble with the three re-entering the country, I was very nervous about the possibility that *The Times* article had activated Special Branch and I was not going to get my clients out of Heathrow that day. As a precaution, I telephoned Gareth Peirce, an experienced lawyer who I could call in an emergency if the worst happened.

When I turned up at the airport to meet the three men, I realised we had attracted a full turnout of the press. Journalists and photographers mobbed the arrivals barrier. The scheduled time for arrivals from Cairo passed. Other passengers came and went, but no sign of our clients. The press grew increasingly impatient. I managed to get through the barrier and went inside to find out what was going on. Customs Officials told me the three had been detained by Special Branch. I asked to see a Special Branch representative and then returned briefly to the press to explain there had been a slight delay and I was trying to clear things up. I find it hard enough to maintain a calm exterior when panicking inside, but at this stage the panic factor had gone off the scale. This was a thoroughly new situation for me.

A Special Branch constable came to see me at the barrier, and explained the problem. They needed to put some questions to the men, but all three refused to talk. It seemed that the Foreign Office had not cleared them. Certainly no FCO representative had turned up at the airport. I tried to telephone the appropriate contact at the

FCO. She wasn't available. It was still only 8.30am. I knew I had to reach my clients and try to clear the situation. When I mentioned this to the constable she agreed to take me through. As we approached a number of senior customs officials, she said, 'Carry on, don't mind them,' and we walked right past. The Special Branch officer in charge explained to me that in view of the publicity they really had to interview the men and get some answers, but he was very happy for me to see my clients. We had never met each other before but their families had explained all about me and my organisation and I was grateful that they trusted me. I asked them individually the usual question before allowing an interview. 'Have we anything to hide?' They were quite emphatic they had nothing to hide and were happy for the interviews to take place without me. I returned to the public side of the barrier to confront an even more impatient press, whom I had just left stewing for a further hour. Thirty minutes later, the three men finally penetrated the barrier to a deafening noise from assorted journalists, supporters and well-wishers, and greeted their relieved families. Reza Pankhurst brandished his copy of the Holy Qur'an aloft and shouted 'God is great!'

During his time in prison, Maajid Nawaz had changed his views on extremist Muslim organisations, such as Hizb ut-Tahrir. In 2008 he became director and founding member of the Quilliam Foundation, an organisation he set up to act as a think tank to combat Islamist extremism. He became extremely high profile and early on addressed the Association of Chief Police Officers' (ACPO) conference on tackling extremism. His former colleagues in Hizb ut-Tahrir regarded him as a traitor.

His experiences also made him want to become a lawyer. He completed a law degree on his return and also took a Masters in Political Theory at the London School of Economics. He had hoped to take up a place at the College of Law in order to qualify as a solicitor.

In February 2008 he telephoned me in some distress and asked for my help. The Solicitors' Regulation Authority had informed him that he did not fit the criteria to train as a lawyer. One of the reasons why he was turned down was that he had taken longer than the accepted period to complete his law degree. The SRA adjudicator ruled that 'the interruption in his studies was entirely voluntary... by knowingly engaging in political activities whilst in a country in which those activities were banned, he placed himself at risk of arrest and imprisonment'. The other ground for this decision was that by reason of his former membership of Hizb ut-Tahrir he was not a fit and proper person to become a solicitor.

I was furious when I heard his tale. The Law Society had taken the view on the legality of his detention in Egypt which accepted the unlawful decision that the organisation had been banned by Egypt. What was much worse in my eyes was the McCarthyite basis for the 'fit and proper person' test. It would appear that if you were, or had ever been, a member of the cult, that fact would automatically exclude you from membership. At this time, Hizb ut-Tahrir was still legal in the UK and I was aware of other members of the cult who were practising solicitors! Maajid also told me he had filed an appeal for a review and The Law Society was out of time for a response. Clearly something had to be done to re-educate those heading up The Law Society.

Maajid agreed that we should approach Duncan Campbell of *The Guardian* and get some publicity for this outrageous decision. If nothing else it should wake The Law Society powers-that-be to the situation and get an accelerated hearing of the appeal. I contacted Duncan and told him that if The Law Society did not think better of its decision I would publicly resign my membership, since I did not want to be associated with a professional body that behaved in such a prejudiced and discriminatory fashion. A couple of days later a great article appeared in *The Guardian*. The Law Society instantly woke up and contacted Maajid to appoint a date for the appeal. Maajid asked me to represent him but I advised him to go to another solicitor since I would act as a witness for him. I recommended my old mentor Sir Geoffrey Bindman and we all turned up together for the appeal. In the event I wasn't needed as a witness and the appeal was successful.

I interviewed Maajid Nawaz in February 2013. I made the appointment through his PA, and turned up in a jacket. He collected me at reception and looked very well groomed with a smart van Dyck beard.

We had lunch at the British Museum, probably the most civilised setting for an interview I had enjoyed so far. I asked him to describe what had changed in his life since leaving prison. I knew about his torture experiences whilst in prison but his ideological conversion from Muslimism – which he now regards as fascism – to liberal democracy whilst still maintaining his religious beliefs is truly extraordinary.

'I have got to say it started with the interest that Fair Trials Abroad and Amnesty International showed in my case whilst I was in prison. It was the first time people I thought of as my idealistic enemies fought for my human rights. As I documented in my autobiography (*Radical*, published by WH Allen, 2012) it fostered a personal journey in me. It started my personal humanisation. I spent four years in prison during which I studied and read books. I'm someone who likes to question. This is why I probably joined the group where I started (the Muslim group Hizb ut-Tahrir). I don't like following social norms. I like to make up my own mind and imprisonment gave me a chance to do this. What I found was that militant Islamism had much in common with fascism. With a background of law, I considered Sharia law, which of course has many interpretations and no single code, and thought it was quite wrong to impose it... When I was released it still took me a further ten months to break with the organisation. Such an organisation becomes one's own identity. I knew my resignation would lead to stigmatisation and a break with members of my family such as my brother. I had to take my time and move carefully, so eventually when I did leave on 1st March, 2007, it destroyed and proceeded directly to the eventual dissolution of my marriage.'

I commented that it was so sad that his personal price was so heavy. I remembered prophesying to him, based on the experience of so many other victims, that his marriage was likely to break under the strain. Victims come back changed and things are never quite the same again. He told me he recorded my advice in the autobiography and didn't believe it at the time.

'I don't have a criminal record in Britain or Egypt because I was convicted under the political codes, not a criminal one.'

We went on to discuss his experiences in qualifying as a lawyer, how he passed The Law Society's finals after his dispute with it had been resolved, but abandoned qualification to found Quilliam. We also discussed the Scientology aspect of his personal life and how it was smashed when he left the sect. He replied: 'Once I had arrived at the conclusion that Hizb ut-Tahrir was a fascist organisation advocating violence, the only thing to do was to oppose it at whatever cost.'

Anyone reading his autobiography can read the harrowing details of the mass torture practised in the *lubianka* of Cairo, the head-quarters of the secret police, al-Gihaz. He was personally spared the worst of it, the electric shocks, the beatings and the *strappado* (being strung up by your arms until your shoulders dislocate). One of his fellow Brits was not so lucky because he couldn't speak Arabic and they took that as refusing to answer questions.

There were some extraordinary parallels between his relatively rapid journey to human rights activist and my more leisurely odyssey. He started Quilliam in the back of an old car, usually parked near Russell Square. I started FTA in my son's bedroom, but at least I didn't have to live in it as well! As he said: 'Reading classic English literature did for me what studying Islamic theology couldn't; it forced my mind to grapple with moral dilemmas... I focused on Tolkien's *Lord of the Rings* trilogy, reading it twice over. I couldn't shake the moral paradox that came to embody. Gollum-Sméagol was an evil creature prepared to do anything to get his One Ring back yet, as the story climaxed, it wasn't the hero Frodo who destroyed the ring. As 'evil' Gollum had done before him, Frodo eventually succumbed to the lure of the ring, making a last-ditch attempt to keep it. It was in fact Gollum who pounced at the ring, biting it off Frodo's finger, before accidentally falling to his death in the lava of Mount Doom. An evil character had thus inadvertently achieved the good that the story's hero failed at, and saved the world. This moral complexity began to fascinate me.'

I did exactly the same thing with the same Tolkien trilogy in my first week at Cambridge, all those years before.

Maajid had the same financial problems with Quilliam as I did with FTA but made the mistake of accepting Home Office funding. They withdrew it when he did something they disapproved of.

We finished the meal discussing our identical politics. He had just become a Liberal Democrat candidate and the evening before, party headquarters had contacted him and suggested he put himself forward for the Eastleigh by-election. He remarked he wasn't ready to become an MP yet: Quilliam needed him. A true fellow spirit.

19

European Justice

From the outset of Fair Trials Abroad I was aware of the 'soft' law, originating with the NATO countries and covering Europe. The states involved had ratified the European Convention and were, in theory, bound by the European Court of Human Right's decisions. In 1993, I contacted the Secretariat of the Council of Europe to get some idea of the reason behind the increasing number of pleas for help, based on breaches of the convention, coming from France and Spain. They told me that the enforcement of decisions made by the court was in the hands of civil servants, national representatives of all the signatories to the convention, who met on a biannual basis. There was no independent monitoring at all and no one could remember a decision of the court being enforced by the group.

It was almost a mantra in the early days of FTA that cases make patterns and patterns make policy. By the end of 1994, even though I was not in a position to do deskwork research, my casework was throwing up patterns of discrimination against foreigners in the European Union's legal systems. I was giving what evidence I could to Parliamentary, as well as other, enquiries. To quote a conclusion of the Templeman Enquiry:

There are already threats to civil liberties as a result of the fact that citizens of the European Union do not have equal treatment under the law in each other's jurisdictions.

It was a rapidly growing problem. According to the Foreign Office, the numbers of British nationals held in foreign jails had more than trebled since 1990. By the end of 1994, spurred on by the growth in international travel and business opportunities, 2,000 were held abroad and numbers were still rising. Although no official figures were kept, nearly two thirds of these were thought to be held on drugs charges – three quarters of them in jails across Europe.

When Gudrun Parrasie joined me, there was at last the opportunity to do some deskwork research. We decided to get some idea of the scale of the problems by conducting a survey of the figures retained by the Consular departments of the European Union, getting their estimates of the number of their own nationals in EU prisons, both tried and on remand.

It was a pretty rough and ready operation but we did achieve returns from Austria, Denmark, Eire, Germany, the Netherlands, Spain and the United Kingdom. On population considerations this suggested a minimum of 10,000 EU citizens in each other's prisons and the remand figure was fifty per cent – that is to say, 5,000 citizens on remand and another 5,000 serving a sentence. From other official sources the general figures for prison population in these countries were twenty-five per cent on remand and seventy-five per cent serving their sentences.

We came to the conclusion that because of a universal reluctance to grant bail to foreigners, more than one in five of them would not be in prison had they been natives of the country concerned. The rational basis for this discrimination was the perceived difficulty of getting the foreigner to return to the arresting country for trial. In an early briefing paper I wrote: *It appears that some governments are against collective action on machinery of justice problems because of sovereignty fears. It must be pointed out that sovereignty is a two-way concept. Allegiance to the sovereign has always been dependent on the right to demand and receive protection.*

The obvious problem faced by a foreigner in most jurisdictions is the need for a competent interpretation and translation process, so that the merits of his defence can be made clear to the court. International law is clear that this need must be met as a basic element for a valid trial.

I first came across the problem in practice in the Manchester

United case. Our Turkish lawyer made it clear that the court-appointed interpreter would be rubbish and we would have to find our own. The local interpreter sworn in at trial could not answer simple questions put to him in English and the judge agreed to our substitute. It did not surprise me to find a low standard in Turkey, but my second experience in a foreign court was an eye-opener.

In May 1994 I became the first British lawyer to appear in south-west France as an advocate since the passing of the Single European Act. Doug Belcher was the computer expert who faced a charge in Bayonne, France. I spent an entire morning waiting for the case to come up, discussing problems of English interpretation with the local court interpreter. She was the English teacher in a nearby secondary school and although her English was reasonable, she asked me to guide her through English names for common crimes. She thought manslaughter was a vicious type of homicide involving butchery. It became clear she had received no training in legal vocabulary. She told me that there were no qualifications as such in France for interpreters. A court interpreter was someone recognised by the local court as an interpreter. There was no register as such.

I was getting a flood of Spanish cases with interpretation problems. One case where an eleven-year-old girl was used in court as an interpreter, and several others involving the ubiquitous hotel receptionist.

There was no way to tackle this problem in a systematic way until Sarah joined me in 1995. Sarah's grant under the EU was to look at how communication is handled in individual national legal systems and how far access to justice is achieved.

The feasibility survey consisted of five countries and the objective was to identify the obstacles to a coherent provision of translation and interpreting services. What it revealed was a distressing lack of awareness of the issues on the part of the justice authorities and judges. The introduction of an interpreter immediately converts the proceedings into a tripartite process so that it becomes slow and cumbersome. One judge said: 'Having an interpreter present is an obstruction to the proceedings of the court!'

There was also a lack of appropriate training available for legal interpreters and not least of the problems were low, non competitive-rates of pay.

The European arrangements for evidence were risible, the British response disgraceful. The European convention on Mutual Assistance in Criminal Matters was signed in 1989. It was ratified by Britain in 1990. Probably the worst feature of the convention was that it applied only to willing witnesses. It contained no penalty for non-compliance so injustices both to the accused and to the prosecution, inevitably occurred.

The British Home Office in 1994 had stated that it was overwhelmed with requests for assistance under the convention. It was then handling some 3,200 requests a year for co-operation, some 1,000 of them for service of witness summonses. Every movement of a witness summons took months, sometimes years, to work its way up and down two governments' systems.

The scale of the problem was staggering. At that time, many thousands of requests for information and thousands of witness summons were issued every year in the European Union. From our own Home Office experience, it was likely that most of these summonses were ineffective. Even if only one in ten of these requests concerned a vital witness, up to a thousand miscarriages of justice would occur in any one year from this cause alone.

Investigations by Alan Beith (Liberal Democrat) and Paul Boateng (Labour), the Opposition front-bench spokesmen on Home Affairs, disclosed that Home Office implementation procedures made this bad situation worse. The convention required the foreign court to give the address of the person to be served.

Our government devised a cunning bureaucratic ploy. When requests for summonses didn't have details of the address of the accused, they were returned with an explanation that service had not been possible. If the issuing authority was unable to provide further details but indicated that the nature of the proceedings made the presence of the witness exceptionally important, they would reluctantly try to find and serve the summons on the individual concerned.

In practice, the local police are unlikely to be aware of the accuracy of foreign addresses and the mysterious workings of international conventions. The British Government's method of operating its discretion to shift the onus of further inquiry on to the issuing authority caused intolerable delay at best and must often have led to gross injustice. What the EU governments could not get to grips with was that this crazy system worked both ways. Prosecutors were hampered too!

In the summer of 1996, an intergovernmental conference for the revision of the Treaty of Maastricht had been convened. Justice had been expressly left out of the original treaty. The European Parliament did not have the authority to defend its citizens' rights. The Commission, the executive arm of the EU, had no power even to initiate topics that the all-powerful Council of Ministers would discuss. The Council of Ministers for Justice consisted of the national ministers of each European member state and worked under a unanimity rule, which meant no progress at all.

In the aftermath of Karyn's case, I discussed with a number of MEPs the tragic impotence of the European Court of Human Rights and the need for a new order of enforcement. It was Glyn Ford, Karyn's lead supporter in the European Parliament, who pointed out the unlikelihood of ever getting the UN Convention on Fair Trial implemented on a global basis. However, something might be done with Europe. The first MEP whom I recall agreeing with me on the futility of the ECHR was Geoff Hoon, later to become a prominent member of Tony Blair's Government.

By now FTA had established the informal group of members of the European Parliament. I was commissioned to write my first positional paper for topics to be put before the conference. The chance political friendship between Graham Watson and myself back in the 1970s brought about a strategic alliance in August 1999. I never lost sight of the importance of individual cases, but the minutes of the trustees' meeting that October noted:

*It was increasingly likely that the outcomes of the forthcoming summit...
would provide work for FTA for some 3 to 5 years. An agenda on Civil
Liberties and Justice is being actively pursued and would need programmes of
research, monitoring and evaluation.'*

I obtained their permission to devote half my time to the new
European initiative and the other half to the needs of clients.

All we knew about the Summit referred to in our Trustees'
meeting was that it was due to take place on the 15th/16th October,
1999, in Tampere, Finland. It was a meeting of the all-powerful
Council of Ministers during the Finnish Presidency. The sole business was to be the creation of a 'European Legal Space' – an area of
liberty, security and justice composed of all the member states of the
European Union. I circulated our 'Want List' to all the important
contacts we had. Amongst our recommendations were:

- The provision of competent legal representation at little or
  no charge.
- The provision of competent interpreting and translation
  services where required from the point of first questioning.
- The raising of judicial standards throughout Europe by
  proper training for judges.
- Provisional liberty in the form of Eurobail.

I travelled to Brussels on the eve of the Summit where I met
Antonio Vitorino, the newly appointed Justice Commissioner, only
an hour before he was due to fly to Finland. He proved to be a ball
of fire, very positive on civil rights and wholly in favour of a twin-
track approach embracing liberty and security. He needed an
explanation of the 'Eurobail' concept. The basic idea was that EU
citizens facing trial and the prospect of a long spell on remand in
another member country should be sent back to their home country.
They would then await trial on such terms as their native court saw
fit. It would then be the responsibility of the native country to return
the accused for trial. I explained that in Spain and France especially
there could be a wait of two years between arrest and trial.

When I discussed the details of the 'Want List' I found that Vitorino and Romano Prodi (the President of the European Commission) had already tabled our list on the agenda of the Summit! Heady stuff! Certainly by the time I went home the next day, I felt that Eurobail would feature in the programme and we might well get some of the rest of our Want List as well.

I learned later from the summit Secretariat that the concept of Eurobail had indeed got as far as the draft programme as 'Measure 61' but it was omitted from the final communiqué because the Finnish Presidency did not understand what bail meant. They thought it had the highly restrictive meaning of putting up of sums of money to ensure the accused's attendance at trial. The Finns themselves had no such procedures in their justice system anyway.

The actual communiqué from the conference was a letdown. There was a programme of practical measures to be drawn up by the Commission and presented to the Council of Ministers twelve months hence, at their December 2000 meeting. The conclusions seemed to ignore the issue of civil liberties. Whilst common minimum standards were called for in multilingual documents to be used in cross-border cases, the difficulties faced by the defendant, witnesses and victims who don't speak the language used by the courts were ignored. A system of mutual recognition of judgements was endorsed without any reference to the standards of judicial competence or any other safeguards for the defendants. They also agreed for extradition without formality to be granted in cases of final judgement, even if the trials had taken place *in absentia* and without notice to the accused. I was already expressing my concern on the malign potential of this measure by the summer of 1999 and the Summit had increased my fears.

Throughout 2000 we lobbied the European Parliament, Commission and many national governments, including those holding the six-month Presidency of the Union, to give the minor civil liberties measures indicated in the original programme a decent priority. The European Parliament and the Commission were with us, but the all-powerful Council of Ministers had the final say and when the priorities of the five-year programme were announced in the December Summit, not a single measure for fair trial had made the list.

Prominent in the first programme for the architecture of the European Legal Space was the concept of a European Arrest Warrant. It was an arrest warrant to be limited to specified serious crimes that if issued in any member state would be executed in any other as though it had been issued following the usual procedures in their native court: *'Arrest sans Frontiers'*.

The European Commission were still working out the details of this new measure when the dreadful events of 9/11 panicked the Council of Ministers of Justice to activate it. Originally as an emergency response to terrorist offences, the problem was and is that they also tagged on a list of thirty-two types of ordinary criminal offences that virtually covered the criminal codes of all the member countries. The result was that with the arrival of this EU Arrest Warrant, the rationale for sovereign protection disappeared without any change in the situation. The underlying irrationalities of xeno-phobia and the mutual distrust of each other's legal systems were exposed through numerous examples. To date there has been no substantive progress on the bail question.

On European bail problems, the worst case we came across was in England. In March 1994, a large yacht with a multinational crew docked in Southampton, to be greeted by two reception committees. One of them was an all-British drug-smuggling gang; the other was a squad of customs officials who had caught wind of the exercise. The seven crew members of the yacht were arrested, along with the eight Britons, and eventually sent for trial. All the British men, save the ringleader, were bailed. All the foreigners awaited trial in prison. The most junior of the crew was the ship's cook. Poor Ursula Jansen, a German citizen of previous good character, spent over a year in Holloway prison. Her mental health deteriorated so alar-mingly that a worried probation service official contacted me. At her trial in March 1995 the prosecution did not proceed against her and she was released, as were three other members of the ship's crew.

We had no problem in demonstrating that the international convention for obtaining evidence, already described in the 'known to the police' case, had completely broken down.

The most extraordinary case we had at the time was a hybrid one involving both bail and evidence. Chris Scott, from Birmingham, was accused of rape by a Finnish girl. He spent two-and-a-half years of a four-year remand waiting for evidence to arrive from Finland to Spain. Even in Spain, a case has to proceed to trial within four years from the arrest and without evidence Chris Scott was acquitted. It was the only case I ever conducted from start to final hearing before the European Court of Human rights. His case against the Spanish government for his prolonged detention was won. I was extremely lucky to have had a couple of the best human rights barristers working with me; Keir Starmer, former Director of Public Prosecutions, was led by Edward Fitzgerald QC.

The legal aid arrangements for the European Court of Human Rights were bizarre! If you lost, you were awarded the average rate for lawyers within the Council of Europe area, and since it included all of Eastern Europe, you got the air fares and accommodation in Strasberg, but otherwise made just enough money for a decent lunch after the hearing. But since we won, the costs were awarded to us as though we had fought the case in England and Wales – a difference of tens of thousands of pounds.

For Chris Scott it was a pyrrhic victory. It was discovered that he had left the body of his father hanging in his flat when he fled to Spain. By the time we won in the ECHR he had been convicted of homicide and faced a long spell in a British prison. The European Court in these circumstances did not make a financial award.

We needed a new initiative. Early in 2003, backed by the drive of Caroline Morgan, the Commission for Justice and Home Affairs published a Green Paper (a considered policy document inviting comment from interested groups) that incorporated all our ideas with a very useful suggestion of their own. This was for a standard document to be given to all foreigners arrested in each member state and in all the EU languages, explaining the basics of their national criminal justice system and, in particular, how to get in touch with legal representation.

In private there were many instances of acknowledgement of our major contributions to this Green paper at the very highest levels of the European institutions. Many other legal and professional organisations that had made minor contributions were credited. There was not a single mention of Fair Trials Abroad.

I'm sure this was a deliberate but diplomatic exclusion since it was clear to us that we had made a number of enemies amongst the national governments. It was our insistence on promoting individual rights to justice, in public as well as private.

It would take all of us the next three years to complete the refinement of the Green paper and make it acceptable to the Justice Committee of the European Council. This meant winning over each individual national government. The process involved detailed consideration of the practical promotion of defendants' rights, from arrest to trial.

Luckily for representatives of penurious NGOs, expenses covered standard rail travel or economy flights, meals and a modest hotel. In the past I had always stayed at a cheap B&B, with the pretentious name of The George V. Its location in the flower market area put it on the wrong side of the Grande Place, leaving me a stiff, thirty-minute walk uphill to the European area, where all the meetings took place. My inability to walk uphill after my heart crisis meant that Sarah and I had to move to the cheapest hotels closer to the centre. We couldn't afford to come to Brussels at all unless we were subsidised, so we made sure these meetings coincided with others we needed to attend with MEPs, the Secretariat of the Civil Liberties and Human Rights Committees and other NGOs.

This endless refinement consisted of experts' meetings convened by the Commission. There were perhaps as many as a score of them over the period. The last thing these meetings contained was expertise. The primary objective of them was as a sounding board for each national government's attitude. The experts giving their opinions were mainly Foreign Office civil servants who covered the topic of justice within their mission to Brussels. Generally they had no legal training whatsoever. When the meetings were convened at short notice they were stranded without instructions from specialists back home. Amateur night.

Towards the end of the period, these meetings degenerated from diplomatic charade to sheer farce. The enlargement of the EU from fifteen member states to twenty-seven meant that, whilst there should have been enough seats with audio equipment to enable all those invited to have the benefit of simultaneous translation, the committee rooms weren't properly equipped for the numbers. Those NGOs, including us, who actually knew what they were talking about, were relegated to chairs around the perimeters without the essential equipment. Unless the national delegates spoke English or French, few of us could understand what was going on.

The very worst meeting I attended was on my specialist topic of bail. Notice was given during the Brussels institutional summer vocation and we convened a week afterwards. Few government representatives knew anything about the topic. The Commission had funded a bail research project in which professional bodies from three different states had cooperated. One of them was the UK. Not only did the other two prove ignorant of their own bail arrangements, they were unaware of the project.

The main thrust of our European justice campaign was to ensure that all states participating in the European Legal Space had suitable facilities for actually implementing the rights guaranteed under the European Convention. We knew that unless there was a monitoring system no progress would be made. In a landmark decision twenty years' earlier, the European Court of Human Rights had stated in the course of judgement: *The European Convention on Human Rights is intended to guarantee not rights that are theoretical or illusory, but rights that are practical and effective.*

In 2002, the commission set up a 'network of experts', one from each state, to devise and report back on the compliance with the European convention on human rights generally, from state to state. The experts selected for this exercise were academics, and there was no one on the panel representing our interest in practical criminal justice. At the end of the first year in 2003, a voluminous report was submitted to the Commission stating that the only practical method of proceeding further was to be by priority themes. One of them was to be Criminal Justice.

In 2004, the European Council considered a Cinderella project by the Austrian Presidency, to set up a European Monitoring Centre in Vienna, dealing with racism and xenophobia. It had minimal staff, and did little to justify its existence. The Council decided to broaden the remit of the centre and converted it to a fundamental rights' agency. It was considered that the agency should also establish in the course of time an authoritative insight into cross-border issues. The Commission stated that:

The agency should be a 'crossroad facilitating contact between the different players in the field of fundamental rights, allowing synergies and increasing dialogues between all concerned'.

In other words, a talking shop.

As we pointed out:

The monitoring services are the touchstone of the resolve of the Union's institutions to ensure that fundamental rights of its citizens are observed. There must be in this context the general concern that the agency may have insufficient human and financial resources to enable it to provide a practical and effective monitoring service on behalf of the citizens of the EU.

In other words, it won't work.

A conference did take place, in which NGOs with an interest in criminal law were well represented, and the Commission promised to take the representations seriously. However, the initiative fizzled out over the course of the following year.

In 2006, the European Council considered the final draft proposals for legislation on practical defendants' rights as presented to them by the Commission. These consisted of greatly watered-down proposals originally contained in the 2003 Green Paper, and in particular an unworkable and ineffective bail system. The draft legislation was rejected.

20

The Future for Fair Trial

I was at a reception in London with a group of young lawyers from the Baltic States when the conversation turned to corruption in judicial systems. One of them told us a story. 'I was quite recently involved defending a judge on a charge of accepting a bribe. What astonished me was the nature of the bribe. She'd accepted half a pig to arrange an acquittal.'

The anecdote sums up fundamental problems in fair trial. Judicial salaries in relatively poor societies that are so low that pork chops can get 'the children of the rich' out of trouble.

Many of the cases I have already discussed have an element of corruption. Karen would never have been arrested without a bargain between drug squad and drug smugglers. The Manchester United six would have never been imprisoned in Turkey if the hotel owner had not let the police in on his insurance scam. In the Clarke case, there was a six-hour delay between Clarke's arrest and the raid on the warehouse just down the road where he picked up his load: since the warehouse was deserted, the real villains must have been tipped off. In Morocco, the corruption was wholesale, Steve Bryant being only one of scores of foreigners jailed to protect the local arrangements.

A few years ago I wrote an *Observer* article where I considered in which legal settings a foreigner could expect a fair trial. In practice there are perhaps a score of them: a handful in the United States and its Federal courts; the 'Old Commonwealth', i.e. Canada, Australia and New Zealand; Western and Northern Europe; Scandinavia; Germany; Austria and the Netherlands, as well as all legal systems in Great Britain, including Eire.

There are perhaps some surprising omissions in Europe: France and Belgium, where in my experience the presumption of innocence until very recently has been more of a theoretical than a practical concept. In one meeting of our expert panel, the French and Dutch representatives discussed their experience with our case referrals. The Dutch representative said he'd never lost a case referred to him. The French representative said he'd never won one.

Transparency International, the Berlin-based global non-profit group, which studies corruption around the world, published the result of a survey in September 2013. After surveying 114,000 people across 107 countries, the group found in what country locals have the least amount of trust in institutions meant to protect them. In thirty-six countries, respondents said they viewed the police as the most corrupt; twenty countries saw the judiciary as the worst. It also found that twenty-seven per cent of people interviewed admitted to having paid a bribe to a member of a public service or institution in the past twelve months. And more than half of respondents believed corruption had worsened over the past two years. As they concluded in another report: *Corruption is undermining justice in many parts of the world, denying victims and the accused the basic human right to a fair and impartial trial.*

Every year the same organisation publishes a ranking order list for perceived corruption in public services.

The ranking orders (least corrupt first) for those in my *Observer* list were as follows:

Denmark Finland and New Zealand equal 1st; Australia 7th; Canada and the Netherlands 9th; Germany 13th; United Kingdom; 17th; United States 19th; Eire 25th.

By contrast, those not on that list: Spain 30th; Poland 33rd; Italy 72nd; Czech Republic 54th; Romania 66th; Bulgaria 75th; Greece 94th; and, outside Europe, Thailand 88th; India 94th; with Russia 133rd.

The corruption index is the only relevant index we have on judicial standards, which is why I've adopted it. An unquantifiable factor that comes through the casework is judicial xenophobia. This was particularly obvious in Kevin Sloan's treatment in Tenerife and Garry Mann's trial in Portugal. It also surfaced in the planespotters case as Greek paranoia over Turkish spies, and the Spanish courts' reluctance to accept British evidence in Steve Toplass's case.

Outside Europe, it is hard to envisage any country joining the band of those who give fair trial to foreigners within the foreseeable future. In order to give such guarantees judicial and law enforcement agencies need to be relatively free of corruption, and this facet of society would appear to take at least a generation to eradicate. There the only changes during my watch where there was any progress were through casework and they were minor, although Rachel McGee's case forced a change in the Cuban justice system to prevent conflict-of-interest through the monopoly of representation.

Another was the case of Rosemarie Morley. Rosemarie was arrested in July 1997 at Karachi airport, with 2.8 kilos of heroin concealed in her suitcase. She pleaded guilty at her trial and was sentenced to three-and-a-half years' imprisonment. In December 1998 she was due for release, having served a prison sentence with full remission. It was then that her case came to our attention. The only time we would support a guilty prisoner is where the sentence passed on them was manifestly excessive, compared to those handed down to that nation's citizens, and then we would only support an appeal on sentence. What was wrong with Rosemarie's case was that the prosecuting authorities were proposing, under new legislation passed after her offence, to recharge her under the new legislation, which carried far heavier penalties and she was facing a further ten years in prison. The cunning ploy was to charge her with possession, as distinct from smuggling, on exactly the same facts. There is no one more protected from legal abuse under International Law than a prisoner who, having been found guilty and served their sentence, faces a further charge on identical facts. With the support of the Pakistan Human Rights organisation we took up Rosemarie's cause in the Lahore Court of Appeal and won. This not only got Rosemarie released, but a score of other Europeans and over 300 Pakistani prisoners.

There is an international code for defendants' rights to fair trial, virtually identical to the European Convention of Human Rights, governed by treaty and supervised by the United Nations Human Rights Committee. The International Convention on Civil and Political Rights (ICCPR) Article 14 recognises and protects a right to justice and a fair trial. Article 14.1 establishes the ground rules: everyone must be equal before the courts, and any hearing must take place in open court before a competent, independent and impartial tribunal. The rest of the article imposes specific and detailed obligations around the process of criminal trials in order to protect the rights of the accused and the right to a fair trial. It establishes the presumption of innocence and forbids double jeopardy. It requires that those convicted of a crime be allowed to appeal to a higher tribunal, and requires victims of a miscarriage of justice to be compensated. It establishes rights to a speedy trial, to counsel, against self-incrimination, and for the accused to be present and call and examine witnesses. And yet in practice the only states that adhere to the code are the same states mentioned in the *Observer* article.

The fundamental flaw is not only that it is a consent-based process but also that the mechanism relies on member states to implement ICCPR standards. And, if implementing ICCPR principles into domestic law would conflict with existing policy or law, a state may ignore such a principle!

Then there is the delay in making reports and consideration by the committee. In its 2006 Annual Report, the committee listed a number of countries overdue in reporting – for example, Gambia (twenty-one years overdue) and Equatorial Guinea (seventeen years overdue).

Inside the European Legal Space the prospect is much brighter. The European Council has produced a roadmap for practical implementation of defendants' rights and has already adopted measures guaranteeing interpretation, translation, provision of a document setting out foreigners' rights in their own language, and access to a lawyer. But the variable geometry of rights to fair trial even in the European legal space will take generations to eradicate.

The influence of a state-controlled judiciary lingers on for up to two generations from democratisation. In countries with career judges, the new democracies start with all the judges having been appointed by the old regime and the most junior of them remaining within the system, becoming more senior, until retirement. In 2005, a local lawyer advised me to drag out an appeal in Spain because the Franco-appointed president of the court would be retiring shortly.

There is also the problem of reality as opposed to lip service. In the decade between Hobbs and Mills and the Michael Shields cases, Bulgaria has joined the European Union and incorporated the fair trials provision of the European Convention of Human Rights into its constitution. The presiding judge throughout the Shields trial was constantly asking the prosecutor whether the protocol had been observed. By which she obviously meant had the fair trials provisions been observed. However through the actual manipulation of evidence and judgement it was a fair trial in form and a show trial in practice.

The real judicial crisis within Europe is much more urgent than that. By the panic measures of 9/11, the European Council established a Kafka-esque arrest warrant system, which practically guaranteed the innocent would be convicted in over half the member states. The result is what I feared and publicly warned against a decade ago. In 2002/3 I embarked on an international tour of legal gatherings in Germany, Italy and Holland. I warned of the dangers of innocent citizens, accustomed to the guarantees of defendants' rights in their justice systems, being absorbed by a sausage machine spewing them out into countries in eastern and southern Europe, where acquittal of foreigners was unheard of. There are damage limitation moves within both national governments and European institutions which will take a number of years to work out. The pity of it is that the arrest warrant with appropriate safeguards is and always has been a vital measure.

So how can we protect victims of injustice in the short and medium term? The best civil society can do is to pressurise governments in those states where rights to fair trial are taken seriously to employ their diplomatic services to support their citizens.

It is not enough that there has been a violation of human rights. Since most countries in the world do not give foreigners a fair trial it would be hopelessly impracticable. The British government alone has over a thousand citizens facing trial overseas at any one time. The requirement must also be that their case has clear merits that have been overlooked. This double test was always my personal criterion for support.

What is required is for the Consular services to work in partnership with organisations such as Fair Trials International or competent lawyers who can evaluate evidence. The Dutch Consular service have as an official adviser a defence lawyer who has close associations to FTI. There are a few great lawyers in corrupt legal systems. But the lawyers who defended Karen Henderson in Russia, or Maitre Suad Lazarac in Morocco, cannot operate effectively without Consular support.

One of the great lessons of Guantánamo was the effectiveness of the pan-European approach. Each government attempted in vain to negotiate on behalf of their own citizens. The exception was the Belgian government, who abandoned their own two citizens.

The creation of a Foreign Minister for the European Union and the establishment of diplomatic representation outside Europe should be developed to include European Consular representation, with a Consular Minister for the Union.

Epilogue

Over the entrance to England's central criminal court is part of a biblical definition of a righteous judge: *He shall keep the simple folk by their right, defend the children of the poor, and punish the wrong doer.*

This definition in retrospect was perhaps the major thread in my life – a thread that began when I was a schoolboy in 1951 through a chance meeting with magistrate Basil Henriques, continued in politics during my young adulthood and on into my work as a professional lawyer in neighbourhood law centres. The thread wove its way deep into the pragmatic road I travelled to create a unique human rights charity.

To repeat my aphorism you start with the casework because cases make patterns and patterns make policy. That is why this book is mainly a chronicle of victims and rescue attempts.

The rich and their children can always buy protection – in June 1995 Patrick Heath, a grandson of Harold Macmillan, managed to jump bail in India at a time when no one received bail on serious drugs charge. Life can be very unfair, which is all the more reason why we should strive to restore the balance.

I was often asked about our success rate. It was always relatively low. I have written here about many of my failures, the two Steves, (Toplass and Bryant), Alan John Davies, Kevan Sloan, Terry Daniels and the Egyptian Three. So what use were we?

I started something and my successors have built on what I started. They have kept the faith, as you can see from these words from Fair Trials International to supporters in October 2013: *As with all our work, our involvement in real cases of injustice is at the heart of this campaign.*

The mission statement is: *Working for a world where every person's right to a fair trial is respected, whatever their nationality, wherever they are accused.*

About ten years ago, in a conversation with the senior lawyer from Amnesty International, he told me he thought that in twenty years we would be to fair trial what Amnesty was then to human rights. I think they are on track.

Throughout my watch I was firefighting. I was totally unaware I was living out the basics of the universal fairytale, from being taken out of a traditional lawyers' comfort zone by Karyn Smith – an unlikely maiden in distress – to facing the challenges from the ogre of bureaucratic indifference. In my middle-aged adventure I learned what Basil Henriques might have added to his words, 'You are as privileged as I was, or you would not be here listening to me. It is our duty to plough something back.'

He might have carried on: 'You will find both purpose and fulfilment… and if you are very lucky, you will have made a difference as well.'

Index

INDEX